Believe

Journey from Jacksonville

Ken Norton
John V. Amodeo
and Donald Hennessey Jr.

1st WORLD
PUBLISHING

Believe:
Journey from Jacksonville

Ken Norton, John V. Amodeo, and Donald Hennessey Jr.

© Ken Norton, Donald Hennessey Jr.,
and John Amodeo 2009

Published by 1stWorld Publishing
1100 North 4th St., Fairfield, Iowa 52556
tel: 641-209-5000 • fax: 641-209-3001
web: www.1stworldpublishing.com

First Edition

LCCN: 2009936293
SoftCover ISBN: 978-1-4218-9120-0
HardCover ISBN: 978-1-4218-9119-4
eBook ISBN: 978-1-4218-9121-7

To our parents who mean so much.

John and Ruth Norton

Don and Marguerite Hennessey

Vincent and Florence Amodeo

IN MEMORY OF

Meagan Jo Hollingshead
October 13, 1988--
May 22, 2003

Meagan Jo Hollingshead:

During class at her middle school in Cedar Rapids, IA, one week before 8th grade graduation, one day before the 8th grade dance, witnessed by dozens of classmates, and without any trained adults present, 14 year old Meagan was killed in a senseless accident involving an Iowa Electrathon, a local high school team car .

Meagan was a champion for children and animals, she was passionate about making changes in the world, Meagan wanted their voices heard. Her life ended that day, but her dreams and spirit live on in those of us having had the privilege of knowing her, and in the hearts and minds of the many lives she touched.

Rest In Peace Baby Girl, Your Free Now! No Pain, No Suffering! As Free as the Butterfly.

FOREWORD

Dr. Don Hennessey, Corporate Manager of Ken Norton Enterprises, called me in late 2007 to consider helping write a biography on the ex-heavyweight champion. Such an endeavor would be a challenge, but one that I embraced and accepted. Given this task involved meeting Mr. Norton, his companion, Rose Conant and a host of other people without whom the book would not have been completed.

Don Hennessey and his mother, Marguerite, were very cordial and helped arrange the first meeting with Ken Norton at his home in Orange County, California. His steadfast and professional demeanor, along with his partner, Daryl Renken, made the initial visit to Mr. Norton's at once a rewarding and memorable experience. What followed was a series of meetings, phone calls, emails, visit to 'Fight Night' in Washington, DC and constant revisions to the text that ultimately became the biography, *Believe.*

Don and I want to give special thanks to Tom Tousey, who edited much of the text and gave us some insights as to style and imagery. We are especially grateful for his time and efforts.

Friends and families in NYC, Jacksonville, Illinois and Mechanicville, offered relevant suggestions to make the story of Ken Norton an informed narrative. A note of thanks especially to Ed Krajewski, Carol Krajewski, Linda Gulli, Dr. Louis Gioia, Wesly Cooper, Fr. Owen Lafferty, Lee Collings, Jerry Adam and Amos Moore, Jr., Daryl Renken, Marguerite

Hennessey, Bill Hennessey, Eva Williams, Linda Christian, Crystal Hennessey, We Love you all.

Jeff at the International Boxing Hall of Fame was very generous with his time and forwarded valuable information on the induction into the Hall of Fame of Ken Norton in 1992.

To all of you, a most heartfelt thanks is in order!

John V. Amodeo/Dr. Donald Hennessey Jr.

CONTENTS

Chapter 1

"What the mind can conceive, the body can achieve."

—Napoleon Hill

Ken Norton was about to face his biggest opponent. This opponent was different. Very different. Instead of a familiar opponent eyeballing him before a throng of packed fans in an arena before a bout, this opponent was much more formidable, testing his every move. An opponent who would try him beyond any of his memorable boxing events. Ken Norton, the self-assured, cocky ex-world heavyweight champ, who had triumphed before an adoring boxing world and had given so much to his beloved sport, found himself in life's ultimate challenge. The opponent had rendered him speechless, immobile and hooked up to tubes in both arms in an environment totally foreign and frightening. Unlike the swift moves in the ring, the only movement around him was the constant, steady drip of fluids. Fluids that were keeping him alive while the constant din of machines checking his vitals were the only sounds heard. There was no easy way out with this opponent. What's worst is that no one, not even the once-feared Norton had any control over this situation. For this opponent was about to take him to a place he had never known and was stepping into the ring with him, like it or not. With a mind of its own, its wrath could not be ignored and brushed off. It had that in-your-face attitude and it demanded respect. Making a spectacle of itself, that attitude was now ready to overcome Ken Norton and declare victory. For Norton, it was decision time—would he allow this opponent to rule? Norton, the champ, knew he was facing life's biggest challenger—give up or keep fighting? He knew the answer, his family, friends and doctors did as well —Ken Norton would knock out this opponent and show him who's boss.

In a 2000 autobiography, coauthored by Marshall Terrill and Mike Fitzgerald, *Going the Distance,* Norton explains:

"I knew from the looks, all the looks—doctors, my sons and daughter, that it wasn't good," Ken remembers. "My body was my meal ticket and now it was trying me." Indeed, family and friends ushered into the intensive care unit, saw the famous patient a shadow of his former self.

Others interviewed in the autobiography gave their own grim assessments.

"What made it especially difficult," his daughter Kenisha said, was "he was covered from head to toe in bandages. Bandages! His jaw was wired, making any communication with us impossible." She went on to say that "the doctors said because of brain injury, he may never walk again." For Kenisha and her three brothers, this was their worst nightmare. The strong dynamo they called Dad was now in great need. "It was hard to look him in the eye. I didn't want him to see the fear in my eyes. My body was shaking just thinking of what was to become of this. This was my daddy and I couldn't do anything for him."

Would he be a vegetable, strapped to some wheelchair with assisted living? Would he be able to talk or walk again? Sudden and unexpected events in our lives can bring joy or sorrow. It's the bad things that we like to forget, but this episode would not go away and the family, like Ken, had to face it head on and decide what course to follow.

What brought about this catastrophic incident occurred on a normal day, Washington's Birthday, February 22, 1986. Normally, a pleasant day. A holiday for the nation's schools and a testament to the father of our country. But this Washington's Birthday was going to change Ken Norton's life forever.

Norton, the champ from small-town Jacksonville, Illinois, who had done his hometown proud and was now living the good life in Orange County in Southern California was asked to attend a fund raiser given by Tom Bradley, erstwhile mayor of Los Angeles. Bradley, a favorite of the media and Hollywood crowd, distinguished himself as the first African-American mayor of the state's largest city. With gubernatorial ambitions, he was destined for stardom in the political world. Would he become the first black governor of California? Like most politicians, he had aspirations for higher office. Being the governor of the most populous state, would automatically put him into contention for an even higher office. Where would he go? He was ready and he wanted to have on hand his good friend, Ken Norton. His chance of winning the Democratic gubernatorial nomination was all but a certainty. What Bradley needed was support and he knew Norton was a man of his word and would assist him in this historic break through. Norton was one of Bradley's favorites. A single father who had raised his son Ken Jr. while struggling in the boxing world, Bradley saw in Ken a person of pride, determination and honesty. He was also a good and loyal friend. The two tall superpowers—one a hard-working and well-liked mayor dressed 'to the nines' in his tux, and the other, the respected, handsome, smooth-talking ex champ who had, like Bradley, achieved the pinnacle of power by his talent and drive. So it was that at the fund-raiser, he would introduce his special friend, Ken Norton, the heavyweight champion who had distinguished himself with the 1977 Father of the Year Award. In fact, Norton, pointed out to the mayor, "I won it twice!" For Norton, family was an important part of his life from his small Illinois town to the big time. He never forgot or gave up on family. He made do for his son during the lean years and now, at the pinnacle of his career, it was paying off with the nation's second largest city's mayor honoring him. As the first African American to be awarded this coveted prize, it was all the more important. The award he was given years before was just as prestigious as the belt he earned in the ring beating Ali.

"That award said volumes and was a wake-up call for all those fathers who had abandoned their responsibilities," Norton remarked. He was glad to be there now to return the favor for an old friend in need, the Honorable Mayor Bradley of Los Angeles, a very decent and hardworking mayor, who was in a struggle. The first African-American governor? Was it possible? Norton was there when he was needed and Bradley needed all the help one could muster.

"I stayed at the Bradley fund-raiser at the downtown Biltmore Hilton. I had just one glass of red wine. Just one," Norton recalled. "Any other beverage was just plain old water, that's it."

As with most fund-raisers, speeches were made, acquaintances were united and good food served. The linen table clothes, the tuxedoed waiters and the floral decorations all added to a night of festivities and elegance. Lots of gossip. Hollywood gossip, political gossip, just nosy gossip. What else does one talk about at these events?

"About 11 p.m. I left, wishing the mayor well and got into my 1978 Mercedes Clenet Excalibur and headed towards the Santa Monica Freeway. I don't remember what happened next."

What happened next would change his life forever.

What is known is that the California Highway Patrol responded to an accident as a result of a young girl hearing the enormous racket created by Norton's car going off the highway ramp and plunging into a steep ravine, hitting a tree. This nameless youngster had the foresight to get her parents to call 911 and within a few minutes EMS personnel as well as LAPD were on the scene.

"This 10 year-old found me upside down, bleeding badly. I never did find out who she was. She might have been a gift from God himself, perhaps my own guardian angel. I think she saved my life," Norton recalled later. To this day, the young girl has never surfaced despite efforts to locate her. Some events have no logical explanation—this was one that, for Norton, was a godsend.

"Just what was a 10 year-old doing outside at 11:00 p.m.? Who was she and where is she today?" Life has unexplained events and this was one that proved a life saver for Ken Norton.

"I often think of this young girl now and imagine her to be an adult, perhaps a mother, a working professional. Does she realize what her presence meant? That the action she took saved me? I wish I could thank her even today."

It was not meant to be. More pertinent issues were at hand and soon to unfold.

Arriving at the scene, Los Angeles police officer Manuel Avila remarked to the *Chicago Sun Times* in an interview a day later, "It was bad, very bad. We had to use the Jaws of Life and then medivac him to Cedars Sinai via helicopter." Avila thought the passenger couldn't have survived and was amazed to see Norton, upside down and bleeding badly, barely alive. The terrain was very thick with shrubbery. Norton later recalled, "If that young girl hadn't gotten help, I would have died unseen in that thick brush." Again, so much was owed to the mysterious young lady.

Indeed, the ravine that Norton's car plunged into was steep and covered with shrubbery; the thick desert-like shrubbery that makes the California landscape both at once picturesque and treacherous. That same dry, thick shrubbery that often catches fire and with devastating Santa Ana winds destroys lives and property throughout the arid West. One moment a photographic scene; the next an unexplained inferno, causing such heartache, millions of dollars in loss and memories forever scarred. Normally, something to be shunned and overlooked. This same shrubbery, however, was so thick that it nearly obscured the car. In an ironic twist of fate, first responders felt that the thick vegetation actually helped Norton to survive, 'grabbing' the vehicle as it fell. Like the young girl, something didn't want to give up on Ken Norton.

"Had it not been for that brush, I probably would have gone down the deep, dark ravine and not been found for days." The thick, desert-like brush plus the young girl's sensible reaction saved the day for Ken Norton. Again, some events cannot be explained.

Avila, one of the first on the scene, recalls in horror what he came upon—an upside-down luxury car spilling gas and billowing smoke from far below.

"That terrible stench of gasoline was there too, a constant reminder that the car could incinerate its occupant.

The Jaws of Life proved essential and critical and the medi-vac unit was right there within minutes," recalls Avila.

Added to the mix was not only the all familiar stench of gasoline but also the urgent necessity of saving a life. This meant swift and prompt action. But the acrid smoke, the gasoline and the debris—not just bits and pieces of metal but chunks of what was once the luxury, eye-catching automobile now a heap of scrap—enclosed its occupant and tested anyone who drew near. Like an enemy combatant, it was at once a source of awe and fear. It had trapped the famous boxer. Its determination to win the fight was clearly evident. Every minute was crucial to ensure that the once prized vehicle not serve as a death trap. The Jaws of Life came though. At least this part of the bout was over.

As with any sudden and life-threatening injuries, time is crucial. So it was on this otherwise laid-back holiday all the resources available stepped up to the plate and got Norton to Cedars Sinai on time.

Rushed into surgery that lasted well over three hours, Norton was then placed into intensive care and remained at the sprawling Los Angeles facility for the next four weeks. Available only to closest family and friends, the famous patient started to rally.

It was day to day for a while, but the doctors were amazed at the tenacious and tough famous patient.

Ron Wise, hospital spokesman remembers: "He came through the surgery very well." Hospital personnel, from the surgeons, nurses and aides who had come in contact with Ken Norton had saved his life. The injuries he sustained would have probably killed a weaker individual. Those injuries could have proven fatal. But this was Ken Norton, the man who wouldn't give up and now showed his resolve once again. Norton had a broken jaw, skull fracture and was strapped to the table like some psycho after a frightened nurse recalled him trying and succeeding to get up, further injuring an already fractured leg. Wise, like the rest of the staff, knew that the prize fighter would not only be in for the fight of his life but also would have to make adjustments to a totally new and strange world. Knowing the gravity of it all, he had Norton wheeled into a private room where those arriving family members could avail themselves with minimum interruptions. Wise knew that Ken Norton would have a rough time ahead. A very rough road for a very active and in-charge kind of guy.

Norton needed not just a wake-up call to remind him that the event off the freeway had changed his total dynamic. It meant a life-changing situation that would test the resolve of anyone, making them aware of the new circumstances that would dictate his life thereafter. Would he be able to endure and, more importantly, accept this new, strange and dependent lifestyle?

"When I woke up from the surgery," Norton recalls, "I was placed in a private room. My family had been notified and was arriving, but I was unable to respond due to the heavy sedation from the surgery. Being strapped up, I thought for a moment that I was in the nuthouse."

"What the hell are these straps for? Why can't I move? Is this someone's cruel joke?"

In fact, Norton had not a clue where he was and what happened. As with many accident victims, the facts become a blur, the incident itself is taken away, for better or worse, and the person is totally unaware of the magnitude of the event. Time and again we have heard of frustrated patients who cannot recall the events that led them to a similar situation. Added to the mix is the difficulty that investigators have to endure when a sole occupant, surviving a near fatality, is devoid of the facts and unaware of what landed them into this state. This is what happened to Ken. To this day, he doesn't recall the events of that fateful night.

"The hospital told my wife Jackie that I was in serious but stable condition," and that "I would face a long recovery with necessary assistance."

Necessary assistance! All his life Norton was in control and now he was in the biggest fight of his career.

Out of surgery and still groggy, he looked at this strange, new environment, wondering what was going on. For the first time in his life, the pugilist, known as the Black Hercules, was in dire need.

"All I recall was the barren walls, the drip of the IVs and that hospital smell—so unlike anything else. Nothing like that in my gym. Smelled more like Lysol or disinfectant. My son Ken Jr. says that I was screaming in pain as I came to." Indeed, Ken Norton, Jr., a junior at UCLA, was beyond reproach when he caught sight of his famous, hero father.

"When the doctors told me that he might not make it, I knew it couldn't be."

"Walking into the room, I knew from the sight of seeing him in that condition that it was going to be totally different." How different no one realized at the time, as the body takes its healing one day at a time, even for the likes of Ken Norton. Ken Jr.'s quick assessment was, in fact, right on target. The accident and its aftermath were staring everyone down and would not be ignored.

"We all have heroes in life; my dad was a superhero. He was larger than life to me. Looking at him in that wretched state, all I could think of was—what now; what can we do;

where do we go from here?"

For Ken Jr., this episode was an emotional roller coaster. This was the man who, as a single father, raised him under the most trying times as his dad was just starting out as a professional boxer. This was the man who made sure he was fed, checked on his school work, prepared dinners and gave counsel. He was a mother and father at once and a person who never gave up while pursuing his dream. These are the things we remember most in life; the hard times, the sacrifices, the lean years and the tough times. Ken Jr., like most of his family, knew that the man in the bed in the intensive care unit was no ordinary man. Yet, this would not be an easy go.

Life would never be the same for anyone in Ken Norton's world. His wife, children and most especially, Ken Norton himself would have to face this challenge and not let it overpower him. Would he be up to the task? Anyone who knew Norton didn't need to ask. He was never a quitter. He wouldn't be one now. Like it or not, he was ready.

Norton, at age 42, was, up until the time of the accident, a man in great shape. That rugged physique, which he attributes to good genes on his dad's side, helped sustain him throughout the four weeks of hospitalization and the many months of therapy ahead.

"I was blessed with good genes; it got me through high school as an athlete in all sports, especially track and football."

"I wanted to walk, talk and be back to my old self again," he recalls. "I was never dependent on anyone else and now this episode came along."

"The thing that bothered me the most was the inability to communicate." Due to the severe brain injury, he tried hard to speak. But it wasn't going to be easy and yet Ken was determined to try. Gesturing, pointing and eye contact were tried, usually to no avail.

"When I did speak, it sounded clear to me, but not to anyone else." He recalls looking around the hospital room and trying to speak of the simple objects there—the tray used for meals and his pills, the leather chair nearby for arriving visitors, the blanched walls with no pictures and the curtain drawn whenever he needed to be changed. Norton's world was typical of what anyone who has spent time in a hospital bed sees—the coming and going of nurses, the announcements for staff to report to some unit, daily evaluation of attending surgeons, and doctors, orderlies changing linen and the cafeteria tray with its aluminum covered plate consisting of very plain, soft foods once the jaw started to heal.

"I'd see the chair adjacent to the hospital bed and would say the word 'chair' to myself." Objects in the hospital room such as beds, chairs, mirrors and sinks became the focus of his determination to speak. Gesturing to family, friends and staff was not enough. He wanted to verbalize. He wanted to speak. Life's simplest inabilities suddenly became a major hurdle. Much like a young toddler wanted to touch and grasp all within his reach, Ken's goal was to let himself and those within earshot know he was trying to communicate. Words suddenly became his challenge and he was determined to utter a word, a sound and a complete sentence.

Life's ups and downs test our resolve and now it was up to Norton not to let this setback overwhelm him. No way would he surrender and be a vegetable. The lack of speech coming out of his mouth was just one barrier that he needed desperately to overcome and he set out to do just that.

"I couldn't speak and it was horrible. This was especially frustrating when my kids came into the room and I just wanted to utter a few words." Ken realized the little things in life that make our relationships so special—a pat on the shoulder for a job well done, a smile to reassure a friend that all was not lost, the gentle yet caring touch of a loved one. Not being able to express your feelings or emotions is hard in normal situations. It happens to all of us, such as the occasional embarrassment when traveling overseas to a remote village where no one speaks English and your only recourse of action is by gesturing or miming out what you need. You try and hope and pray that the person understands. But this was far different and far more foreboding. The accident that landed Ken Norton in the hospital for a month-long stay made it all the more difficult. Yet, this was Ken Norton, the champ the world loved, the actor who broke racial barriers in 'Mandingo' and 'Drum' and the father who raised his son to professional status and three Superbowls. The challenge was within himself and he knew he had to be his toughest critic. Like the stranger in a strange land, he was no longer in command. Yet, he wanted to learn the rules and fit in. Others might justifiably succumb to the ravages of the accident, allowing the situation to at once engulf and capture their body and soul and seek pity. Others might descend into a dark cloud of despair and depression, angry at a God that placed them in a now-dependent state. Still others would use this tragic episode and not let it absorb and conquer their body or spirit. That was Ken Norton's mantra to 'never give up' and get back to life. He would start, however difficult it may be, but he would never, never surrender. Like Churchill rallying the British people in the midst of the great Blitz of World War II over London, Norton rallied his family and by sheer determination and willpower he would show them and the rest of the world that this setback would not be the end.

It would be the beginning of a long, fearful and treacherous journey. The journey would take him, like the traveler, to a strange and difficult world, testing his every move. Yet he was determined to get started. Getting out of bed was the first step and he was ready to meet the test. There was no doubt that he was up to it.

What made the situation more difficult was Ken's desire not only to get up but also to walk to the chair in the hospital room and sit for a few minutes. Norton had entered a new phase in his life and he knew he would have to give it his all.

"I never gave up in the ring and I wasn't about to now."

So it came to this—fight this new fight and don't look back. Face the new reality, the new life that fate had thrust upon him. Where to start? How do I cope? He wasn't sure of this new journey, but he was up to the task and like any good fighter, was ready to meet his challenger head on.

Chapter 2

Starting over can be a painful experience. Everyone has had episodes in their lives that profoundly test their faith and resolve: the sudden loss of a loved one, necessary surgery, loneliness and withdrawal from family and friends as a result of love gone bad. Weaker individuals may succumb to the bottle or prescribed drugs and languish alone. Feeling unwanted and afraid, the mind takes over and those within earshot are suspect as the person withdraws further into oblivion. Today's television viewers are barraged with ads for these pills. A panacea for any ailment from depression and insomnia to erectile dysfunction. But no pill or combination of pharmaceutical miracles that greatly assist with depression can replace the human need to survive and overcome these obstacles, to feel whole again. With time, we learn to adapt and move on and not look back, as hard as the hurt may be. Yet, the invisible scars may remain and test us from time to time, but, like a good soldier, we carry on. We leave the devastated battle scene. The sights, smells, noise and acres upon acres of depleted landscape against a gray sky constantly undermine us. Give up and let loose! But we don't. We're too strong for that last humiliation. We try not to look back, holding up our head and leaving the scarred landscape of devastation, its foul odors of death fading with each step. Pain, hurt and despair can be conquered. Often it comes with a price. That price can isolate the person, withdrawing him or her resulting in permanent distrust or anger. Yet there's always a way out of our deepest and darkest moments.

Like a strong soldier leaving the battlefield, we move on. Sometimes it takes an understanding shoulder or a professional who can walk you through the tunnel and see the light. But not all changes can be temporary. When the change is physical and catastrophic, testing our very fiber and will to live, the result is a life-altering experience. Those scars are there for everyone to see. A person disfigured as a result of a fire, an illness resulting in amputation of an infected arm, injury in the Iraqi desert, sudden blindness or a permanent limp are all fears that no one wants to contemplate. Ken Norton's new life after the accident of February 22nd, was now that of a vulnerable, injured and scarred person. Despite his Herculean strength and impressive physical stature, he was now a person in need. Great need. How to adapt and be whole again? Could he do it? Would he do it? Where to begin?

The people closest to him made all the difference. People in his life both past and present were there in person and in spirit. Like anyone in such a predicament, he needed help.

"I was 52 pounds lighter, my vocal cords were still not functioning, the entire right side of my body was paralyzed and to add insult to injury, my jaw was wired shut." Looking in the mirror was no easy chore either. "I had to face the fact that everything—everything had changed."

Norton knew how Ali must have felt after his stunning defeat by Ken, resulting in a broken jaw for the garrulous Mohamed Ali. "Imagine someone finally got Ali to shut up!" In a bizarre twist of fate, he now knew the agony Ali went through as a result of the 1973 bout. The motor mouth Ali was not able to speak and all due to Norton's now famous jab. Yes, it was an ironic twist of fate, the gladiator of the ring was now the person with the wired jaw! Ken Norton was the man with the broken jaw. That broken jaw, as devastating as it was, was just one of the major medical problems now confronting him. Worse was the inability to take a step unaided. The paralyzed right side wouldn't allow him to move one foot against the other. The prospect of never walking was a veritable reality; a very painful wake-up call. It was now or never and Norton knew the challenge would be unlike any he had encountered in the ring. But he was ready to begin. He had no choice. After all, this was Ken Norton, and Ken Norton never backed down from a challenge and he was not about to let this one have its way. Never!

Like most patients, Norton wanted desperately to do the things we take for granted—walk, talk, take a bite of food on his own and get on with his life. It was these same simple things that would be by far the most daunting and difficult for him.

The 'little things' in life suddenly became not so little but a challenge.

"I was always in control. My body was my meal ticket. For the first time in my life, I had to depend upon others just to get by." Proud and uncompromising in most circumstances, Ken Norton was a person in need. Now, a man in need of assistance and reaching out just to perform daily, ordinary routines. For any ordinary 42 year old, the challenges of the accident would test anyone's will and pride. The former world champion, whom millions admired, wishing they could possess his same talents, strengths and movement in the ring, was now a patient who would have to make a choice and accept the challenges destiny brought forth that February night.

A proud person doesn't like to admit to errors. A proud person wants to show the world that he's capable of anything. Yet too much pride can be deadly.

This was one hell of a wake-up call. Where was he to begin?

"I had to depend upon others to feed me, clothe me and take me to the bathroom."

For the first time in his life, Norton had to face the facts: he was in need of assisted living and had to take a big piece of humble pie. Change is never easy. The events of the accident made the changes permanent. Daily routines would now be replaced by the decisions of others. Simple things like dressing, shaving and eating were now major hurdles that had to be in the hands of family and therapists. Depression, loneliness and a feeling that you're no longer useful can set in. Many times people surrender to their emotions, allowing the insecurity, fear and denial of the new order to take hold. These feelings can overwhelm a person and further erode their progress to recovery. But Ken Norton was going the full distance and not surrendering—"I was never a quitter and I'm not one now." Changes had to occur and change became the direction to recovery. Where to begin? It began with a new schedule.

Schedules revolved around his progress: appointment dates with therapists, progress follow-up interviews with family, lists of 'dos' and 'don'ts' to ensure his safety. No longer able to drive, dress himself and meet with friends, Ken had to come to terms with himself. He was never a quitter and now, in his biggest crisis, he wouldn't allow circumstances to take over. He thought of his childhood and his morning Cheerios and bananas and longed for them more than anything. A connection to the past and to the future. Like an old friend, that big box of cereal was on the shelf looking at him like some past opponent in the ring. A box of cereal!

"As my jaw healed, that box of Cheerios suddenly became my first hurdle. My first chance to get back my life.

I was determined and stared at that box and knew I would conquer it.

"I remember my daily breakfasts before the accident; as a kid I always ate Cheerios and bananas. Took them for granted. They were part of my growing up that stayed with me even when I was champ. I never realized how much those Cheerios and bananas meant to me!" To this day, they remain his staple breakfast diet. Cheerios and bananas!

As with other patients who had to make the transition to assisted-care, Ken Norton was determined, like some religious zealot, to adhere faithfully to the regimens imposed upon him and to make strides. Where was he to begin?

Ken Norton had to make the painful leap and realize that he was no longer a totally independent and mobile individual. Now a person in need, he remembers the traumatic transition.

"When they placed that handicapped sticker in the car, I felt violated. Me, Ken Norton now reduced to a cripple! I often saw the handicapped space and, on occasion, would see a person jump out of the car. Handicapped or just lazy? Now, however, just staring at the sticker was a jolt of reality." he recalled. The anger and fear that all of us face was now about to take over Norton and overwhelm him. Or was it? Where to begin?

Ken's anger was short lived, however. Over the next weeks, months and years, he gathered his boxer instinct and became a loyal and dedicated patient, determined to prove to himself and anyone else that he would triumph. He would walk, talk and drive and be an important asset to his family and many friends. He would not despair or brood over his misfortune. Instead he would muster all his strength and show everyone he was ready to start anew. Once again, the world would get to know Ken Norton. A different Ken Norton for sure. More important, he was ready to show himself that he would not give up or surrender. He would become a model for anyone in such similar predicaments. Determined, aggressive and never a quitter, his boxing instincts learned so well from his managers would now take center stage. Was he up to it? No one really ever doubted his resolve. Least of all Ken Norton himself. He was ready for the test.

"I was like a new building coming up, piece by piece."

Like a new structure about to grace the skyline, it had to start somewhere. There had to be a plan, a blueprint, a map that would show direction and steady, yet encouraging progress. The mind started to work and Norton's awe of the construction of huge skyscrapers suddenly became real. He would be not the same Ken Norton, but he was determined to show anyone within reach that he could build himself back up and be on his feet again. Like a new structure, he would rise up, a new Phoenix and a new, albeit wounded self.

Ken would be that new building, making sure that with each passing day a new part would be added. Brick by brick, mortar by mortar, he was ready for the challenge.

"Do you ever walk by a construction site and see the intensity of the workcrew?" Each day progress is made, especially putting up a 50 or 60-story skyscraper. Norton likened his progress to a building, starting from scratch and bit by bit, you one day see the beginnings of what will be gracing the skyline and boldly demanding respect. Like the buildings, he would take it day by day, making incremental progress and grow in strength and resolve.

"I often marveled at all facets of a building from the

excavation to dynamiting solid concrete to get a foundation. Then, the steel girders going up with the cranes pushing higher and higher and adding floors with each passing day. The movement of the crane, almost like an acrobatic balancing act." Slowly at first the building takes on a character all its own and prides itself as a tribute to the multi-tasking of the construction crew. A crew identifiable by the familiar hard hats worn, proudly asserting to anyone within shouting distance that the monument erected will in part, be their own legacy, serving as a monument to their labor and skills. Like the ancient Egyptians' masterful and awe-inspiring pyramids that endured the test of time, the modern building becomes a source of intense pride. Pride to its workers and the city whose skyline it will grace for all to see for miles. Pride to the architects who have a unique and inspiring vision. Pride to the many corporations who call it home. Pride to the workforce from the service and maintenance personnel to the executives and secretaries who can point out to visiting friends, "That's where I work." One can marvel at the infrastructure, such as the miles of pipes whose job will be to carry water and heat; electrical wires that will allow it to sparkle against the sky and the windows to complete the job. Yet the entire structure is nothing without the work, sweat and know-how of the crew from the architects to the worker with the muddy shoes and soiled jacket mixing the accurate load of concrete for all of the floors. Floor by floor, with each one complete as it soars to the heavens, the building takes on its own personality. Each job is as important as the next and the entire team, working in harmony, will be a team undefeated and undeterred. The end result is a wonderment to the world, proclaiming its stake to the city's genius. From the daily procession of passers by, the building's progress becomes, for some, the common topic at the water cooler and for tourists, a photo-op and treasure of a lifetime.

Looking up and taking photos for posterity, the building embraces all within miles as the modern pyramid of its day.

"Sometimes I would just sit there, staring at the 14 steps that led up to the second floor bedroom, wondering if I could make it up to the second step. I had to literally do things one step at a time!"

Ken Norton's home was a constant reminder of his triumphs in the ring. An area set aside was a repository for any boxing enthusiast. One wall had photos from the famous fights that the world knew—the 1973 fight with Ali in San Diego, the return bout in 1976 at Yankee Stadium, the heavyweight belt plus the trophies and citations from the boxing world. Also, pictures from the 20 movies he'd made from the steamy sex scene in 'Mandingo' to later films, such as 'Knight Rider,' 'Dirty Work' and 'Oceans of Fire.' The fighter's biggest challenge now was to move from a wheelchair to a walker and then walk entirely on his own. The 14 Steps became like a Hitchcock drama, making him a real actor. Reality replaced drama and the actor and fighter became one. Ken knew he was about to face the most challenging role in his career. Where to begin? Looking back in his wheelchair at the 'shrine' of his accomplishments in the ring and on the screen, he was determined to persevere. Norton was never in doubt and he would overcome this obstacle regardless of what doctors, family and skeptics told him. The scrappy young man from the Midwest was going to overcome and again, no one would be in his way!

"Those 14 Steps were not just a means to an end. It was my way of proving to myself that I could do it, get the job done and not let the wheelchair dictate my life."

Norton's determination was clearly evident within a matter of days. Despite the grueling pain and ever-present danger of losing his balance, he started his steady climb. His steady climb, ever moving up and not looking down, making it step by step, day by day and getting himself back.

Norton's quest came at a price. It would take two years to climb the entire length of 14 steps and reach the second landing. Each day, inch by inch, holding onto the banister and forcing his leg to move when it didn't want to.

"One day I just sat there in the wheelchair and looked upon the stairs as I would look upon a challenger in the ring. It was a script straight out of 'Rocky.'" Unlike the Stallone blockbuster movie that won the young Stallone the Oscar for best picture, Ken Norton's 'Rocky' was the real deal. With the discipline he learned in the ring, the stairs became his entire life, taxing his resolve and challenging him to the max. Yet, it was a goal to be reached and one that he was not going to lose.

"No way were those stairs going to dictate my life. They represented a challenge and I glared at them with the same intensity that I would an opponent about to face round one. My mind was focused and clear. I knew what the deal was."

The 'deal' was to get up from the wheelchair.

"All that jump roping in the gym made my legs still strong at 42 and I kept telling myself that it was time to do the move." What Ken Norton did was just short of miraculous. He had astonished his doctors and family by coming through the accident and now it was time to show who was boss. The regimen of therapy was coupled with the mental intensity that he had learned in the ring.

"Use your mind, focus on the event and get it done." With this simple yet powerful message he was able, slowly at first and with each passing day, to gain a little more movement in his leg. Within a few months, he was able to stand and hold on and then move on to a walker.

"I never gave up on myself and I knew deep inside that I had what it takes to get over."

Indeed, Norton's instincts took over and with the daily regimen of therapy and lots of love from family and friends, he was able to set out and conquer his biggest obstacle.

Two long years! Rehab. Constant routine, continuous struggle. Never give up.

Each step conquered was a celebration. With therapy involving massages and swimming, he slowly got back the strength in his legs. Despite the paralysis on the right side, he was able to move his leg regardless of the pain. What his doctors, family and fans saw was what Ken had always had inside—a strong, determined resolve not to give in but face the challenger, whoever it was, head-on and deal the winning punch. From his earliest years as a young man, the lessons he learned from his Aunt Mary, parents, coaches and friends never left him. Others in a similar situation may have given up or been bitter and asked: 'Why me?' Instead, Ken got his strength from others and in turn, it would make him an advocate for others in similar situations.

"That's what it was like to me. Making progress day by day, inch by inch and finally conquering." The building blocks were now in place, the plans laid out and Ken Norton was ready, like a building soaring to the heavens, to pick up and begin his journey. A journey that had taken him so far from that small Illinois town.

Chapter 3

Jacksonville, Illinois, the county seat of Morgan County, had at its last count in the 2000 census a population of 19,000. A typical Midwest town, just 60 miles east of St. Louis, the city has, according to the census, a median age of 37 and a racial composition that is 90% white, 7% African American and the remainder Latino or Asian. The average income of $45,595 is typical of most American households and Jacksonville is still today a typical Mid-American town as it was at the time that Ken Norton was growing up.

Like every city, Jacksonville has a history. What makes this small city unique is that it is home to two colleges: Illinois Central and MacMurray as well as four state-run institutions including the prestigious Illinois School for the Visually Impaired and not so prestigious Jacksonville Correctional Center. Also in the city are the Jacksonville Developmental Center, a former state hospital and the Lincoln Land Community College's Western Regional Center. It also proudly boasts of having a daily newspaper, *Jacksonville Journal-Courier*, the state's oldest continuously published newspaper since its first issue in 1830.

To any youngster who attended a state fair or had been on carnival rides or to the now more common Six Flags or Great Adventure Amusement Parks, a connection to Jacksonville may not be obvious except to the workers at Eli Bridge Company. Eli, the manufacturer of Ferris Wheels and other popular rides, such as the Scrambler, has been a part of the labor force since W.E. Sullivan founded the firm in 1900 with the first big Ferris Wheel, which he proudly displayed on the city's square that same year. It remains there still. So it is that many a youngster or teenager shared their first date, first kiss and first taste of freedom riding the American carnival's main attraction. Seen from a distance, with its colorful lights, it was a place for a young man to meet friends, swap stories and plan an evening at the fair while tasting the cotton candy and looking at the girls. The sights and smells of the midway were centered around the majestic, tall and imposing Ferris Wheel. It signified power and strength and yet was so beautiful. Those beautiful colored lights were unlike anything seen before by a young, impressionable, small-town kid in an America that was far more innocent and secure. Its height stood out for all to see at once beckoning to anyone to defy its power and test its resolve. A meeting place, a sight to behold, it was what made the fair so magical. The Ferris Wheel! With cotton candy in hand, you didn't think twice and before your senses took hold, you had a ticket or two in your hand for this great machine. So what if the sticky cotton candy got on your shirt. Mom would be there when you got home to clean it. You had to hold on for dear life up there above the trees. It was worth the risk. There would always be an excuse you would create. Yes, it was the Ferris Wheel where stories yet untold would begin and your view of the familiar surroundings seemed so different up there. Your imagination would take over and up there a different world challenged you to look beyond your young years and out to the bigger world. Your first taste of freedom. Your sense of awe and power. A carnival without a Ferris Wheel? What would Christmas be like without Santa or Easter without the bunny? Like these celebrated icons, it endures to this day as it did for your father and grandfather before him. Yes, a great deal is owed to Mr. Sullivan and his strangely alluring contraption. Yet, without it, a fair would be incomplete and the multitudes would be deprived of one of life's momentary yet great escapes. Soaring upward and giving anyone a sense of wonderment, power and freedom, it was pure joy and amazement. The music, smells of hot pretzels and hot dogs and the sounds of The Ink Spots, The Platters and Billie Holliday in 1950's America were put on hold. They had to be. It was the Ferris Wheel that lured us, made us feel grown up for the first time in our young lives. Yes, we owe much to the Jacksonville men and women at Eli who over the years have brought us so much of that joy and helped us discover ourselves in the process. Many of us got to know what must lie beyond by taking that ride. That inevitable plunge on life's journey. Our first big taste of what was to come. Oh what a ride it was the first time up—what a ride!

A young Ken Norton would have seen the tribute to Mr. Sullivan's invention known as 'Big Eli Wheel,' on the corner of East Morton and South Main Streets. Like many young people growing up in Jacksonville, Ken Norton probably just passed by it on the way to school or going to the ball park or track field. Like most Jacksonville youngsters, he was more concerned about his athletic feats and the girls watching on the sidelines. Unaware of its historical significance, the monument to Sullivan was just a site on the square and a place on the way. Yet it was part of the landscape and a tribute to the genius of one of the city's many important figures. Norton was also part of the curiosity and was not to be deprived of the Ferris Wheel's allure. But, like most natives, young and old, he took the unusual monument at East Morton and South Main for granted. For a history buff, however, Jacksonville was replete with many episodes in the young nation. A microcosm of the greater area it was surrounded by, its geographic location made it a focal point in the nation's troubled past. For escaping slaves, it was a haven and way station on the road to freedom—the famous Underground Railroad itself went through the heart of this gallant Midwest town.

The Morgan County Historical Society of the Underground Railroad Committee on Gierke Lane is proud of its purchase of the old Huffaker farm, which served as a way station on the Underground Railroad. That too is part of Jacksonville's past. In a February 9, 2004 article by Greg Olsen in the *Jacksonville Journal-Courier*, he cited Kentucky-born owner Michael Huffaker as hiring "fugitive slaves to run his extensive grain, cattle and horse farm." The article went on to say, "Michael's farm was one of the safest stations on the route from Jacksonville to Springfield. If blood-hounds were being used, the refugees, once reaching Jacksonville, would be taken to a nearby brook, sometimes through the famous tunnels in town, follow the brook to the Mauvaisterre, leave the creek where it branched into Michael's farm and there, sheltered by the orchard, safely reach the house or one of the cabins. If the danger was too great, they were rushed on to the next station." The idyllic setting and the tranquil pace of the farm kept suspecting federal agents from really knowing what was going on. Olsen further cites local historian Ensley Moore who said of Huffaker, "He was a valuable man for the Underground Railroad because he was fearless, won everyone's respect and never talked!" What courage it took to house, shelter and defy the Fugitive Slave Law and give refuge to those so much in need. Imagine, being silent on such a momentous issue and making sure that frightened runaway slaves kept quiet as well, lest they end up back in bondage and Huffaker in federal hands. Yes, Mr. Huffaker's farm is embedded in the fabric of the American journey. Little did he know that his bold, courageous stance allowed so many a chance. A simple chance to survive and be free. So the little town played a major role in the nation's darkest hour. A most important role. The fact that it's preserved so well is a tribute to the Morgan County Historical Society.

Although overshadowed today by its larger and younger sister city in Florida, Jacksonville was the real deal. It was named for the nation's colorful and contrary seventh president, Andrew Jackson. President Jackson was a controversial albeit successful military leader who triumphed at the Battle of New Orleans which resulted in the deaths of nearly 2,000 British soldiers fighting in the old European formation against the rag tag army of freed blacks, frontiersmen, native Cree and Cherokee and Louisiana pirates fighting a guerrilla war. The same Jackson that later went on to become the first 'common' president in 1828. He epitomized the Western spirit that would resonate well with the people of the town who named it for him. He was a true populist in the Western tradition who hated Wall Street and Big Business and blamed the press for the untimely death of his beloved Rachel prior to his inauguration. That Western spirit was part of the makeup of the early settlers that would make Jacksonville compete with its nearby city, Springfield, for capital of the state.

And, of course, it served well in antebellum America as that important way station for the Underground Railroad. With its location, just east of the slave state of Missouri, runaway slaves would find a haven in the city's churches in free Illinois and the Huffaker farm, offering them a refuge from the treacherous journey to freedom. To a person held in bondage, the freedom that awaited them was far more challenging than the future generations of Jacksonville's young riding the Ferris Wheel and feeling free. The tunnels and brooks surrounding the Huffaker farm made it an ideal escape route. Yet, their journey was life-challenging, replete with fears and reprisals and the possibility of returning to bondage. Jacksonville to them was the Promised Land and a chance to liberate oneself. Freedom. The chance to be oneself. The chance to start anew. Jacksonville was indeed the Promised Land and Huffaker was their Moses.

The city is proud that one of its most prominent citizens, US Senator Stephen A. Douglas, the author of the controversial Kansas-Nebraska Act in 1854 and the concept of popular sovereignty, was admitted to the bar in Jacksonville. It was the same Douglas who paired-up with an obscure fellow-Illinois congressman from nearby Springfield, Abraham Lincoln, in a series of senatorial debates in 1858. Debates that became the catalyst and model for the quadrennial presidential debates of the 20th century beginning with the now famous Kennedy-Nixon race in 1960 and all future ones that have since ensued. The Lincoln-Douglas Debates, seven in all, throughout the state, questioned the slave issue and allowed Lincoln and Douglas to challenge each other over the future of the divided country and, in turn, introduced Lincoln to the national stage. It was a coming out party for Lincoln who showed his deft intellect at Freeport that challenged Douglas over his pet issue of popular sovereignty despite the recent and devastating Dred Scott Decision by the Supreme Court a year before. This decision allowed the spread of slavery not only in the territories acquired by the Mexican War but also throughout the nation. Chief Justice Taney, a slave owner from Maryland, rendered the death knell for abolitionists when he wrote: "Slaves are property and can be taken anywhere." Abolitionists throughout America were at once repulsed and crushed. The tension was exacerbated by the decision and made the ensuing conflict inevitable. Illinois would play a major role.

Despite Douglas' triumph in the senate race in 1858, Lincoln's reputation was born and the two were once again matched in 1860 on the national scene with far different results. Like a boxer in the ring, Lincoln would win this time. Not a knockout, but a TKO. With a divided party of Northern and Southern Democrats, the Northern Democrat Douglas lost to the Republican Lincoln and the nation's 16th President was elected albeit with just 42% of the popular vote. Within months, the nation was a bloodbath, involved in the great Civil War. So, Jacksonville was not just an ordinary town. It played a major role in the nation's history time and again, conflict after conflict. Years later, in 1896, a graduate of the small school of higher learning, Illinois College in Jacksonville, William Jennings Bryan, won the Democratic nomination for President, losing to William McKinley in November. The youngest man ever to win a major party nomination, the youthful Bryan at age 36 catapulted to fame with his now famous 'Cross of Gold' speech which electrified the convention. Thrice defeated, he remained a force in national politics, dying in 1925 after the famous 'Monkey Trial' in Dalton, Tennessee defending fundamentalism and the teaching of creationism. In the now famous exchange shown in the reruns of 'Inherit the Wind', the tired and insolent Bryan met his match in the great lawyer of his day, Chicago's Charles Darrow. Yes, Jacksonville was a very American town but one with a proud past.

What town can boast of three governors: Joseph Duncan, Richard Yates Sr. and Jr.? How many towns have an old haunted former high school? The old Jacksonville High School, like any high school, has a rich history. The Illinois Prairie town has given the folks of Haunting Tours a venue unlike most. While academics and sports were part of the mix, so too the old school was the scene of great loves and heartaches and some speculate, ghosts. So a look at the brochures for the first-time visitor is apt to include a visit to the old grounds, now renovated with an upscale apartment complex. Old stories die hard as do old love affairs. Are there really spirits roaming the premiere apartments? One can only imagine the likes of the old paramours searching in vain for their long lost loves. Hope springs eternal, even in the most unlikeliest of places!

Jacksonville also made the 'Ripley's Believe It or Not' list, as it once boasted four churches on the corner of so aptly named Church and State Streets! A constitutional lawyer would love to have stood on one of those corners. Church and State! One would have witnessed prior to 1968, the Grace United Methodist, Trinity Episcopal, Mt. Emory Baptist and the State Street Presbyterian Churches. Imagine Christmas service and the choices one could make to hear the best choir, the best sermon and witness the best interior holiday decorations. If only those walls could talk. I'm sure the fine ladies in their Sunday best complete with matching dresses and hats made for quite a sight. Maybe on Easter Sundays long gone the competition to 'strut their stuff' made for a great photo op in the next's day edition of the *Journal Courier.* Or worse, if a pastor wasn't up to his usual oratorical skills, all one had to do was to select from the other three! Jacksonville provided its citizens with an array of options, as we have seen from the Ferris Wheel, Underground Railroad and haunted sights to churches juxtaposed on four corners. As fate would have it with old structures, fire and demolitions have now given way to other structures. Condos now stand where stately houses of worship once did. Yet an old aerial photo shows those stately houses of worship so proudly gracing the four corners. If congregants, long gone, could come back and see what has replaced the stately structures, their tough Midwest attitude would undoubtedly kick in and anyone within earshot would be asked why destiny had rendered the corner of State and Church to such a fate.

The small Midwest town was still not done with its cast of characters. With the advent of the 20th century, Jacksonville provided a US senator, Jake Mullen, a mystery writer Wilson Tucker and a host of outstanding sportsmen from pro baseball pitcher, Luther 'Dummy' Taylor to Henry 'Harry' Staley and Olympic water polo bronze medalist, Calvert Strong. Also, Dr. Greene Vardiman Black who had the foresight to introduce to dentistry the first use of 'laughing gas', nitrous oxide. In an interview, shortly before his death in 1915, Dr. Black said, "I wanted to extract teeth without pain." No doubt millions of citizens were also grateful! So, a little American city, nestled in the Illinois prairie was more than just a dot on the map or a stopover on the way to St. Louis or up to Springfield. It was and has remained an integral swatch of the fabric of America and should be justly proud of its citizens who made history and life more bearable. It was host to the famous and others, long forgotten.

However, the most famous son of Jacksonville in the 20th century is Ken Norton.

Chapter 4

Ken Norton, the famed pugilist of his day who would go on to make the city of Jacksonville additionally proud of his accomplishments, came into the world, like everyone does, innocent and unprepared. His birth, however, was not expected nor anticipated. In fact, Norton's introduction to the world was at the time less than stellar and not considered a blessed event. In fact, it was a birth that caused upturned eyebrows and the ensuing gossip of the 'problem.'

Ken's mother, Ruth, was, at the time of his birth in 1943, a 16 year-old out-of-wedlock mother. The biological father was George Florence. Soon out of the picture, Florence left town, leaving the young mother to raise Ken on her own. "That's the way it was in those days," Ruth recalled when interviewed for *Going the Distance*. Without a breadwinner in a small, gossipy town the stigma of an unwed, young mother raising an infant son was a great challenge. Ken's mother's frank assessment of her situation was quoted in the 2000 autobiography. In it she went on to say candidly: "I was only 15 when I became pregnant with Ken. Marriage was out of the question as George, the father, was not much older than me. In those days, if you didn't marry the person, you would have no contact. Nothing. Men didn't come back even to visit. So, George and I went our separate ways. Yet, he lived right down the street when Kenny was growing up. George and Kenny saw each other and often acknowledged one another. Ken knew he was his father, but they had no contact."

The dead-beat father was not even contemplated in those days. If you didn't marry or were too young, you left and went on, even if it was in the same town. That's just the way it was. This episode was duplicated throughout America in the era before the sexual revolution and women's rights organizations. Pity the poor girls who had to 'visit' their far-off aunt and come back alone, never finding out what adoption agency had intervened. Before they realized the scope of what transpired, they were expected to act 'normal' and blend back into their community. Before Planned Parenthood, before consulting and before the intervention of court actions, a young, unwed mother in America had to conform.

This was the America of the 1940's and 1950's.

When Ken speaks of his father, he points out: "He was 6'1" and was both muscular and athletic. A solid man with a solid frame. I heard that he had boxed when he was in the army in World War II. I know one thing he did give me: good genes. My physique I got from my biological father, that's for sure." George Florence was already a big man, even when he fathered his now famous son.

Born on August 9, 1943, Ken Norton was originally named Kenneth Howard Florence. On June 21, 1947, it was changed to Ken Norton as a result of the marriage of his mother to John Norton. John Norton was his dad from that day onward.

"John Norton," Ken proudly boasts, "was my father. Standing a mere 5'7", he was a dynamo." For Norton and his mother, he brought stability, values and most of all love. It was a marriage that lasted and like most, tested the resolve of all involved. Yet to a young Ken, he was his hero, his mentor and the person who showered it all on his beloved son.

Not his biological father, he nevertheless was there throughout his life and was the person that Ken or any young man in his situation would be so fortunate to call 'my dad.'

"My father was a workaholic. Because of him, we never were in need. Mom also worked hard at the local hospital. As an activities director, she got to know much of the happenings in the hospital and the people who made up the staff from the doctors to the orderlies to the maintenance department." It takes a special person to be in that position in a tense often somber environment and the roller-coaster emotions that evolve in a given day in any hospital. Ruth Norton could deal with all kinds of people and was a greeter, advisor and counselor all rolled into one. Her son, Ken benefited from this commitment and was instructed by his parents and his Aunt Mary to always respect others. His mother's strength was the result, as a young mother, of showing how strong she could be in bringing up her son to be the best. She and her husband became the solid fortress for the young, headstrong young man. Ken was given responsibilities from his parents and was blessed with a strong home environment that stressed a sense of fair play and honesty. Strong values like these helped sustain Ken in the toughest times from being a high school athlete, a Marine, and to the pinnacle of power as world heavyweight champion. Indeed, in his darkest days after the accident off the freeway, he drew strength from the people who molded his life and helped him overcome his most challenging event. People like his parents, his Aunt Mary and his high school coach, Al Rosenberger. When he thinks of his childhood, a smile comes across his face.

"I admit I was spoiled as a kid. In large part because I was an only child.

"I did have chores like any kid my age. In the brutal winters, I would get the coal, haul it upstairs to our stove. I got strong from carrying those coals up the wooden stairs. Time after time, I would slip on the ice and fall flat on my ass, but I got up, knowing that was my job. Who would want to be in a house freezing in mid-January with the winds blowing at 40 mph?" Young Ken Norton did get rewarded for his efforts. A cocker spaniel became his constant companion, a gift from his loving parents.

Ken's mother Ruth recalls how his appetite grew as he got bigger and stronger.

"Kenny liked the comfort foods I would prepare for him. That meant a lot of meat and potatoes such as pot roasts, ham and of course, chicken. In the summertime, he loved the barbequed-ribs, chicken and the great desserts. The family gatherings were an important part of our lives. Since I lost my mother so long ago, my Aunt Mary was always there, a strong, positive influence on me and the rest of the family."

In the summer, Ken mowed the grass. "Remember that in the 1950's it was a hand-powered lawn mower. None of those electric lawn mowers. Just sheer muscle power. In the fall, the leaves would cover the front and back of the house. I would rake the lawn, occasionally stopping to talk to neighbors and making sure the girls noticed me. Sometimes I rake over the same spot and even drop leaves and fake it, giving me the excuse to talk to some foxy young females."

Growing up for Ken Norton in Jacksonville in the 1950's was typical of many of middle America's youth. He now had a stable family. As noted, his adoptive father, John Norton, a diminutive man, was a stark contrast to the young Ken Norton. Ken soon towered over his dad by the time he reached his teenage years. A native of Jacksonville, John Norton had met Ruth when she was a young girl from

Missouri. Church events at Mt. Emory Baptist and other socials brought them together and at 18, she and John were an item. Her 1947 marriage sealed a bond that lasted half a century until his death in 2000.

Ruth and John Norton set up house on Hackett Street, just a few doors down from the woman who raised her, Aunt Mary Bell Hill. Ken's parents, his aunt and ultimately his high school coach would have a major impact on his life.

Looking back on his early days, Ken recalls: "We don't appreciate the sacrifices our parents do for us until we're older and many times fail to thank the people who modeled our lives." Ken was a youngster, who unlike many in the boxing world, had a great family, instilling him with a sense of fair play and right and wrong. Norton was surrounded by parents who sacrificed and taught him solid values and respect for others. It molded his character and made him strong, the strength he would later use to overcome challenges not only in the boxing ring but also, and more important in life itself. After the car accident, he reflected often and his thoughts were back in the Jacksonville of his youth and the parents who made him whole.

Yes, Ken was an only child. Without siblings, he was given the things that many in less fortunate situations could only dream. Since he was the only child, he was quite naturally spoiled! Many of his fellow competitors in the ring envied the thought of having a stable and complete family. So many fighters came up under terrible circumstances in neighborhoods rife with drugs, guns and fear. But not Ken Norton. His small town offered him exactly what many of the boxers lacked. "I had my own room, my own bike and toys—I was a happy and wholesome young man." His parents weren't well-off but were hard working and willing to sacrifice things to provide for their son. Like many young people, you don't realize the work it takes to raise a child and instill in him the values that will endure. It would take Ken Norton many years to fully appreciate the parents that made him the man he was to become.

By the time he was 9, in 1952, the third grader started to excel. That year, the Jaycee Junior Olympics sponsored a competition at the Jefferson School. Young Norton entered several events in the field of track: 100 yard dash, the standing broad jump, the long jump and finally the 440 yard relay race with his young buddies. As he cites in his autobiography, *Going the Distance*, "My chest was decorated with the blue ribbons by the end of the day. I knew I was the best athlete at Jeff." Indeed, from that moment the young Ken Norton started to attract attention and more importantly, respect. He went on to say: "That blue ribbon turned my life around. It was a driving force."

"My parents were always there for events that didn't conflict with their work schedules. Seeing my mom there for me was the best incentive. She gave me the drive, the motivation to succeed and make her proud."

Ruth Norton remained by her son's side despite her initial misgivings when the professional boxing world called.

"My mom was my biggest fan and never, never missed any of my bouts but was there in spirit at the arena." For Ruth Norton to see her son in the ring getting hit and pounded was out of the question. No mother wants to witness, however glamorous and spectacular a sight, an event that might be bloody. Instead, she remained in a hotel room, praying that the fight would be over, her son would win and both fighters emerge unhurt. It took special courage for Ruth Norton to stay, sometimes alone in the hotel room while the world was waiting anxiously for the results. For still, this was her baby and Ken Norton, stepping into the ring, knew she was there close by. The fact that his mom was there was a great asset and motivated him even further.

There are seminal events in our lives that move us to change direction, realize our potential and face the consequences. For Ken Norton, that day gave him the confidence in life that would eventually make him a prized athlete in high school in three sports and introduce him to the world of boxing. By the time he reached high school, he was 6'3" and 195 lbs. The coach at the high school, Al Rosenberger, interviewed for his 2000 autobiography summed it up best: "Norton was the best all-around athlete I had ever seen in my 30 years of coaching." Agile, quick on his feet and able to throw a football or run a mile in a track event, he was a dynamo that the local coaches from neighboring high schools learned to respect and awe.

His friends and the girls were always there for him, Ken recalls. "It's amazing the respect you get when you're a young athlete."

Norton was molded by his parents and his Aunt Mary and wasn't an arrogant type.

"I had a temper that had to be controlled. Sports helped me tremendously and gave me a great deal of respect." Indeed, he was recognized on the streets of Jacksonville and both whites and blacks were proud of the local youth who had already made a name for himself. The city was still racially segregated as far as housing and even in local venues, such as the movies, but, as an athlete, he was in a class all by himself. "It felt good, real good."

By 1960, he was a senior star athlete not only in track and football but also basketball. Rosenberger summed it up best in his description in Ken's 2000 autobiography: "His style of running reminded me of the great Jim Brown."

Norton likes to point out that in 1960, his team beat neighboring Beardstown by the incredible score of 74-0! Probably a record for a high school team in Illinois. People start taking note of such talent. The talent that Ken Norton possessed became the subject of local sports columns, coaches and of course, scouts who were out to find a promising athlete for their universities. He had excelled beyond anyone's expectations, especially in track where he entered eight events which caused opposing teams to take notice and eventually get the state of Illinois to pass the so-called 'Norton Rule,' which now limits high school track entry to three events.

Such scores and ability made Norton a prime draft pick. Athletic scholarships came in from many schools: Nebraska, Ohio State, Oklahoma, San Jose State and Iowa to mention a few! Eventually he selected a closer venue, Northeast Missouri State, now known as Truman State in honor of the 33rd president, native Missourian Harry S. Truman.

Sad to say, his career at college was cut short. The parties, girls, and fun-like atmosphere gave way to less than stellar academic grades.

"I was young, naive and having a good time. When I came home to visit, I was told that I had better shape up. My mentor, Coach Rosenberger told me to go back and apply myself and keep my ass in the seat and listen to the lectures."

But his coach's advice was short-lived. By his sophomore year, an injured collarbone that he sustained back home trying to get back at his old girlfriend, resurfaced. "That girlfriend, Gloria, did more than break my heart. Thanks to my stupidity, I pursued her when she was with her new boyfriend. I guess no one likes rejection. I couldn't deal with it and ended up by getting hit by her boyfriend's car! I was too embarrassed to tell anyone, even though it was deliberate.

My pride was compromised. Now I have a permanent reminder of Gloria—real pain in the form of a fractured collarbone. I wasn't about to let anyone know about it and had played football with the pain that came with it. A constant rub-in-your-face from Gloria! Gloria made sure that I had a permanent reminder of her! During my sophomore year at college, I got angry, very angry at the coach. I just had to let off steam. Over something stupid. He just got under my skin and I let off steam. I was young and cocky and not going to let anyone get pissed at me. It happened on the field that morning. That's the day that ended my college football days and scholarship". It ended when Norton exploded at his football coach and walked off the field, showered and abandoned his scholarship and headed home!

Home, as always, was mom, dad and Aunt Mary.

"I had enough of college. I knew my dad would be pissed, but I also knew that mom was there and of course, my Aunt Mary. My sainted Aunt Mary."

Chapter 5

Because both his parents worked, young Ken would be placed in the care of his great-Aunt Mary Bell Hill, who lived just down the street. Ken's mother, Ruth Norton was raised by Mary when Ruth's mother died. Ruth recalls: "Mary was a second mother to me, having lost my mom so young." Indeed, Mary was known to be the person always there, ready to offer advice whether asked or not and ready to warm your heart with a smile and food. Life had dealt Mary a rather sad episode. She had married and her husband was drafted and never came home. It was the war. The First World War. The war that President Woodrow Wilson, said: "Would make the world safe for democracy." Yet for Mary it was the most devastating time of her life. Young Mary, now a widow, lost her husband in the damp trenches in France during World War I. A doughboy who fought with Pershing, he was drafted and left Mary to fend alone with three young children. But misfortune was not finished for the young fatherless children. As fate would have it, the great worldwide outbreak of influenza did not spare Jacksonville. Like towns throughout America, big and small, the agony of war was compounded by the flu that killed millions. It did not spare the house on Hackett Street. All three children died young as a result of the Great Influenza Outbreak in 1918. Mary never remarried. Imagine your entire world disappearing before you—husband and children—family gone. She felt her life was over until she started raising her niece, Ruth, Ken's mom. Ruth Norton's mother had died young and she was in need. Mary stepped in and, despite her overwhelming grief, became the surrogate mother and loving presence for Ken Norton's mother. This was the strength and courage that sustained her and allowed her to carry on. Mary never complained throughout her life and was the bedrock that ultimately gave her young grand-nephew the presence so needed in his life. What strength this woman had!

Left without any husband and children, she became the surrogate mother for the family and doted on all her nieces and nephews. These children would become her new family and give her reason to move on. She loved all of them, but there emerged a favorite from the crowd. A grand nephew. That one nephew who was her real pride and joy was Kenny.

"Everyone should have an Aunt Mary like I did." Ken Norton's grand aunt was the bedrock of his early years. Providing an outlet for him away from his parents, he became her favorite of all the nieces and nephews looked after by the elder relative. Spoiling Kenny, sticking up for him and giving him a sense of freedom while maintaining control was the method Mary used so effectively on her young great-nephew. A surrogate mother, a caretaker and a friend all in one package, she had an enormous effect on the life of the future world champion.

Coming into her house on a cold fall day, the smell of the hot chicken soup from the kitchen, her soft voice asking if he had a good day at school, was just the ideal environment for a young man. Hanging his coat on the rack and starting his homework was part of the routine for young Ken.

"On those cold days, entering the house, wiping my feet on the mat, hanging up my coat, I can still see her at the kitchen stove, aromas of fresh home-made chicken soup and the table set with bread and a glass of milk. Before I could sit, she reminded me to wash my hands. Then, the steaming plate was there, a smiling Aunt Mary, complete with a few stains on her otherwise immaculate apron, reminding me to: 'Eat and get warm.'

"That soup had everything to take the cold snap away: noodles, onions, celery and of course, spices that made your palate water and the fresh chicken meat that had stayed in the pot and was ready to devour."

Eating at his aunt's house was a daily ritual which he often reflected upon.

Young Norton was indeed a lucky man. To have such a doting relative, who got joy from giving, made him sustain later in life the pain and challenges of not only his boxing career but also the post-accident recuperation period. She was a bedrock of strength that, later in life, he was able to appreciate.

"During that period after the accident, both in and out of the hospital and the rehab that followed, I thought of what my aunt must have endured. What she had been through." What his Aunt Mary endured was the agony of diabetes.

Imagine an active, church-going woman who never missed Sunday service at Mt. Emory Baptist Church and walked many blocks to and from church and the store. A woman who never complained and wanted only to please. Here was a woman who had lost everyone in her immediate family—her husband, children—and now was beset by an illness, chronic and unrelenting. A real heroine, who never, ever complained and accepted life's crosses as a divine plan without much control. She was accepting of whatever came her way. What came to her in her last years was the painful onset of diabetes. A disease to this day that plagues many Americans with life-altering consequences. In Mary's case, the diabetes would result in an amputation of one of the once-active lady's legs and render her dependent upon others for the first time in her life. Still, she never uttered a harsh word or asked for help. The illness made her a person in need, something that was foreign to her. For the first time in her life, she was now in need. Tables reversed, it was a hard adjustment for anyone as independent as she. Indeed, after his accident, Norton grew strength from the ordeal of this strong and formidable woman who was now in such pain. His memories of her, however, are ones of love and fondness and they bring a smile to his face even today, some 30 years after her death.

"I can see her even today cooking, hovering over the pot, casually looking at me and reminding me always to wash my hands before I sat at the table. Sitting down at her table was a real treat. Of course, we said grace before eating and her prodding me about school, girls and sports were great conversation topics. Topics that were non-threatening and she asked with curiosity about her young grand nephew and his development into a young and vibrant adult. Good and sound advice and having a lot of faith in God and family." For a young man, this stable figure was the perfect influence.

"I always knew when she would get upset at me. Her frown and eyebrows raised with a few shakes of the head sent out the message that something was not right. She didn't have to say a word. Her face and expression said it all."

Ken recalls: "She didn't have a job; she worked to raise my cousins and me." One can imagine the enormity of the task. Making sure that the young ones had food on the table, finished their homework and had some time to themselves. She was a person who gave orders yet was so beloved by the future heavyweight champ that, to this day, he remembers her fondly, a glint of both sadness and pride in his eyes. For it was Mary who filled the niche that was so essential for a young man curious and ready. Ready for anything.

"I was able to exercise some freedom, play around with my cousins and be a kid," he recalled. "There would always be Aunt Mary to rely on and she would be there. And yes, she would stick up for me when the going got rough with my folks. Aunt Mary won out too!"

Yes, during our lifetimes we can recall those who affected us for better or worse. Your first grade teacher, your coach at the Little League, your buddies on the block, your pastor or priest and of course, your family.

For Ken Norton, Mary played the key role in the formation of a young man.

Living nearby, this most dependable and reliable person was always there. Indeed, Ruth and John Norton knew that their son would be in the best of care. Being fed and entertained by Aunt Mary was an essential part of his life. She didn't have to reprimand her lot; they knew the deal with Aunt Mary. You obeyed her and everything would be fine. In turn, you would have that food on the table and a chance, without parents around, to let loose and be free. It was a time for Ken and his cousins to grow up in a loving and stable environment which was greatly enriched by this gentle soul of Aunt Mary. So much love in that house, so much love.

"Growing up we all have older folks we looked up to or were afraid of or wanted to be around. For me, Aunt Mary was the embodiment of love—always giving and never asking for anything in return. Like most older relatives, she had the time to give to us."

"Holidays, such as Thanksgiving, Christmas and Easter

were the best," Ken recalls. "I still can smell the aroma from the kitchen on Thanksgiving. The sweet potato pies, the pumpkin pie, the gravy and the turkey made it a feast. A sight to behold." Each of us have special events, such as family gatherings on a hot, humid summer day under a backyard tree with plenty of food.

"During the summer, we would eat outside. The tall trees in the back yard were a perfect setting and the breeze provided a great relief from the hot, prairie summers. Of course, it was the cooking I remember. We sometimes forget the little things in life. In the summer, that meant that my friends, family and some of our neighbors would gather and have a picnic. I can still smell the fried chicken, based on her own recipe and seasoned only like she knew how. The potato salad, collard greens and fruit from peaches to watermelon were always there. Friends would come by and talk and talk. Talk was plentiful and of course, after dinner the fellows usually sat under the tree and spoke of the St. Louis Cardinals or the Cubs or White Soxs. The women collected the paper plates, cleaned off the outside wooden table and would come around and ask if everything was ok. Wiping their brows from the hot, humid summer weather, the women, young and old, would then sit like the fellows and dish the dirt on the latest news in town—who was sick, who was 'seeing who' and whether we'd have some relief from the heat. Some of the older folks would fan themselves as they listened to the person speaking, occasionally nodding in agreement or raising an eyebrow if the there were some disagreements. It was fun. It was family. People would take their favorite seat in the lawn and on folding chairs and after eating, snooze a bit or just start talking again. That talking—about anything and everything from baseball to the local happenings at the church and in our own ballpark. We also knew it was a changing world, especially in civil rights."

This was the decade that saw the brutality played out on TV of the murder in Money, Mississippi of young black Chicago native, Emmett Till. The scenes of the crime, the denials of the all-white police force and quick trial and acquittal and the failure of the Eisenhower administration to involve the FBI made America aware of the great divide over race in the country. The same year of the murder, 1955, also saw the successful non-violent boycott led by a young Baptist preacher, Dr. Martin Luther King, Jr. in Montgomery, Alabama. The world was changing and for young Ken Norton and his family the civil rights revolution led by Dr. King and others would have an impact on their lives as they would for the rest of Americans. For the moment, it served as a topic of discussion, fear and concern at those family gatherings under the summer sun shaded by the tree and the love of family. Yet, it was there and wouldn't go away. Sooner or later, cities and towns across America would wake up to the clarion calls of King and others over the injustice. But for young Ken Norton, it was the beginning into adulthood. Political and social events were far removed and not his concern. But right now he was a youngster enjoying the free time before adulthood and surrounded by a family that deeply cared and enjoyed each other. He was a kid having a good time with a support system that was solid and strong.

Ken especially recalls his favorite time of year as a youngster, Christmas.

Christmas was a very special time for the Norton household.

"The tree had the traditional trappings, but there was something else too. The pictures of the family on the bureau next to the tree in the living room and a small but neat nativity scene. Everything was arranged so precisely. The tree had the bulbs, tinsel and lights in order. The small figure adorning the treetop was angelic. But there was always some funny things as well on the tree. I remember the special cards that were placed on some of the branches from relatives both near and far and the special red ornament that her husband had given her so many years ago. Good memories on a tree. That's what Christmas was all about. Those are the things that I treasure the most.

"When she got very sick, I was in the St. Louis bus terminal, ready to make the long ride to Camp Pendleton, California. I was a 20 year-old who never strayed far from home and now in 1964, there I was ready to begin a military career with the marines. The marines—the branch that doesn't mess! So it was with great apprehension and depression that I learned that my aunt wasn't going to make it." Ken's mother had called to explain the situation and luckily for him, the commanding officer allowed the young recruit to head some 100 miles east to Jacksonville.

Ken was able to get to Jacksonville shortly after Mary passed on and was there for her final tribute. When you lose someone close, there are different emotions, fears, doubts and anxieties that go through one's head. For Ken Norton, this was a severe blow. His first very close encounter with death. Like most young people, he was angry and in need.

"I was angry. I don't know at whom or what, I was just angry and felt terrible."

Mary's service was a reflection of her life, full of beautiful hymns with the pastor and family speaking warmly of her, as the ushers and lady escorts came around with fans and saw to it that the family was taken care of. Yet, for young Ken Norton, this was a turning point in his life. He at once felt deprived and although Mary had led a full life and was always a very positive and spiritual force in his life, he was one angry young man. Yes, he knew that she had great faith in the Lord and was now in a better place. Yet, it wasn't enough. Grief does that to us. Before we can come to terms with it, we have the anger, depression and loss of control. This was especially true for a young soon-to-be recruit in the US Marines.

"I thought of my aunt and tried to be positive, but you have to deal with this situation in your own way. I let off some steam after the funeral at the house when family and neighbors came by and started eating, drinking and getting loud. They were grieving in their own way but I thought it was wrong and I set out to let them know. I was angry at this display—thought it was disrespectful. I yelled and carried on until people, feeling uncomfortable, started leaving. This was my way of coming to terms with this situation. I know my aunt would understand my outbursts. When I look back on it now, it's apparent that I was in need of someone to be there for me. Aunt Mary now gone! It just didn't make sense, regardless of her illness, her deteriorating health and loss of a leg. I guess I just didn't want to let go. That's the hardest part, letting go. I was young and not fully in control. My outburst at the house was my way of showing my aunt that I respected her and loved her. Over the years, I look back on this and try to remember the good times growing up in her presence and how much she meant."

All of us have experienced the grief that Ken Norton felt. Some of us wear it well, masking it until we're alone or try to return to work and act normal and yet there's always something missing. It happens to the best and to the richest and poorest and to anyone who had, even as a youngster, a pet dog, cat or hamster die. It's part of life and we learn to move on. Family and friends are there, true, but each of us deals with it in our own way. Time does help. For some of us, we need more time, more space, more isolation and more intro-spection. History and literature are ripe with tragedy

—Romeo and Juliet, West Side Story and all the war movies that end with someone not coming home. For some, like young Teddy Roosevelt who lost his beautiful wife Alice giving birth to their daughter the same day his mother died, isolation and reclusiveness was partly a remedy. Indeed, Teddy's concern for conservation started, in part, by his need to get away from his New York townhouse and travel out west to the Dakota Black Hills. Some good does come from this form of grieving. For Roosevelt, it was travel and the need to explore and be free. He got to respect the land and a keen interest in preserving the environment. His biographer, Edmund Morris in his celebrated Pulitzer Prize winning book, *Theodore Rex*, points out that Roosevelt "never compromised in the area of conservation" as President. Roosevelt also had the money to travel and get away from his home. He had the means to do this and came back to New York City stronger both physically and mentally and ready to honor his mother and wife as a steward of the people. Events, both good and bad ones, have an effect. For young Teddy Roosevelt, it was his reentry into the world and he used it positively to move up the political ladder. With leadership comes scrutiny, but TR was up to the task. His grief was redirected and its impact led him to such venues as the hero of San Juan Hill in the Spanish American War to governor of New York and Vice President with William McKinley in 1900. An assassin's bullet in Buffalo in 1901, made him the youngest occupant of the White House and Morris, in his biography, points out the impact of that time in the Dakota Bad Lands

Much like TR, individuals such as Ken had to cope and move on. Yet, like young TR, Ken Norton was coming into a new environment that would not only mature him as only the marines can but also help launch his meteoric rise in the boxing world. The death of his beloved great aunt and surrogate mother was a turning point in his life and helped him mature to be the strong, resolute man he is today. Much of what we call values and character is given to us to either absorb and grow or cast aside. For Ken Norton, the lessons of life began over that hot stove in the small kitchen that was so much a part of his world. It made him a man and forced him to come to terms with the challenges that awaited him. Everything he would need to sustain himself over the years he learned from the gentle lady in her kitchen pleasing her favorite grand-nephew: respect of oneself and others, gifts of love and laughter and faith in God. "Some people take themselves seriously and end up miserable. My aunt had every reason to be angry at God and the misfortunes that fate bestowed on her. Yet she carried on and made me strong and I'm grateful for her enriching my life." Ken Norton, to this day, thinks of his aunt and a broad smile appears. The gentle lady did indeed mold a man.

Chapter 6

Ken Norton was on his way to Camp Pendleton in Southern California. Founded in 1942, the sprawling marine base is located between San Clemente and Oceanside with over 125,000 acres and 17 miles of coastline along the Pacific. An impressive facility that would awe any first time visitor, it was also the place where young enlistees were sent for the rigors of basic training. By the time young Ken Norton reported for basic training in 1964, it was the largest Marine Corps base in the US and home to the 1st Marine Expeditionary Force and the headquarters for the 1st Marine Division. It was the first time that Norton was so far from his roots in the Midwest.

1964 was also a year that America would remember for the escalation of the far off conflict in the Southeast Asian country of South Vietnam. It was a year that saw troops sent by President Lyndon Johnson involved in an all-out war, albeit an undeclared war against the communist North Vietnamese regime of Ho Chi Minh. Honoring our commitments to the government of South Viet Nam, as outlined in the SEATO treaty agreement signed in 1954, LBJ listened to the Joint Chiefs of Staff and made his decision to deploy American GI's to the far Southeast Asian nation. Timing is everything and this wasn't good timing for Ken Norton. This was the year that the newly-enlisted recruit landed at Pendleton after a long and lonely bus ride following his Aunt Mary's funeral. For the first time, he felt really alone but yet ready to face the challenges of basic training. Would he be one of the "Few and Proud?" Would he live up to the motto: 'Semper Fi?" The long bus ride from St. Louis gave him the chance to reflect.

"Will I end up in Vietnam, getting myself shot? My big self a prime target?" he thought as he glanced at the other passengers, mostly young enlistees on their way to Pendelton.

"I'd look at the window and day dream and wonder 'what the hell am I doing?' I saw the landscape change from the Midwest prairie to the soaring Rockies as we moved across the west. Like any long distance travelers, a lot of guys slept. Others chatted with new friends or read from a book or newspaper. A lot slept. I noticed a few who had trouble making eye contact and peered out the window, each passing moment bringing them to an uncertain future. Scared yet not willing to admit it. I was in the same boat as they were. I wouldn't admit it, too. Wonder what they're thinking about? Home, a girl left behind or just having second thoughts. It was a bit scary, given the situation in the world, but at 21, you think you can handle anything. Think you'll live forever. We didn't know what a mess that Vietnam war was going to be."

Like the other men on that bus, he was venturing into a new and totally different world. What lay ahead?

Traveling to a new destination can be exciting but with an uncertainty of what lay ahead. The men on the bus headed for Pendleton were like the thousands of others, both drafted and enlisted, who would end up headed for combat in a far-off and strange sounding land. It would be an experience that would change their lives and, for those who made it back, would make them men. For others, it was a nightmare, replete with torture, drug use and questioning the government's goals. That would come later. But, right now,

Norton was the young, raw enlistee ready to step up to the plate and give it his best.

"I heard all about the Marines and how tough they were. I was ready and yet not quite sure what lay ahead." He was in for the surprise of his life.

Camp Pendleton would prove to Ken Norton that he was ready for the challenge. As he recalled in his autobiography, *Going the Distance*, "I'd be up at 5AM and try to be the first out of the barracks. I wanted to make a good impression. I had so much energy; wild energy and wanted to show off. I knew what was expected and I got a lot of respect because I was in such great shape the other recruits looked up to me and I became a popular leader. My size, the way I carried myself, my self-confidence all were pluses. Deep down, I knew I had to prove to myself and others I had what it takes. I actually found basic not so bad, even with the crazy, shouting and obscene drill sergeants. At times, I had to suppress my laughter when the drill sergeant shouted the most crazy, bizarre sexual scenarios at us. Sure, you hear guys complaining about the drill sergeant and how tough and in your face he'd be, but I didn't have a problem with it. In fact, I rather enjoyed their strange humor."

What Norton learned from his weeks at basic was responsibility and the need to take charge. It was a lesson that pushed him to the limit both physically and mentally and he passed with flying colors. It also got him ready for events that would change his life.

"Being away from home, having the freedom to make choices and yet get disciplined by tough-talking officers is just what I needed. As I look back on those days in the Marines, I credit them with giving me the source of inner strength badly needed by an angry me at the time which would sustain me throughout my boxing career and post-accident period."

Following basic at Pendleton, Norton was quickly assigned to the other side of the country to Pensacola, Florida.

"Being from the sticks in Illinois, I found that Pendleton and Pensacola, both along the ocean, were ideal for me. I'd walk the beach and listen—listen to the roar of the waves, the breeze blowing in my face and the sun beating down. The warmth from the sun and the noise of the surf hitting the beach was a real turn on. I knew I wanted to be near the ocean and that's why I live in Southern California today, away from the harsh winters and in the great sunlight. I still walk along the beach and sit for a spell along the boardwalks and have my Cheerios and bananas just like old times."

Like Pendleton, he found himself at home in Pensacola with a skill he didn't realize he had acquired.

Surprising himself, he was a quick learner and within a few weeks was working as a radioman, learning Morse code and sending out messages.

"500 words a minute! I surprised myself until I heard that the radiomen are the ones that are usually targeted first in combat.

"I knew as the war in Vietnam was getting worse, it was just a matter of time before I was sent there. With my skills as a radioman, I was certain that I would be one of the first to go.

"There's not much you could do when you're deployed to combat and I just figured my time to go was at hand."

Events were indeed changing rapidly in Vietnam. With the escalation in fighting, every man on the base knew it was just a matter of time before they received orders to go overseas.

"The TV news showed more and more fighting and already there were some demonstrations against the involvement. The war was becoming the issue on America's mind. We knew that the situation was getting worse and wouldn't improve. Being the good soldier and competent radioman, I knew my time was coming." But, Ken Norton was about to have a life-changing experience. And it happened in his native Jacksonville.

"I went home an anxious, highly-driven and horny young man!" And the girls were there. Plenty of them who remembered the outstanding athlete, now even more muscular and alluring to his admirers.

13 weeks later, he was given a furlough to visit family before heading to Camp Lejeune for an almost certain assignment to combat in Vietnam.

"I wanted to see my folks. I figured they'd ship my ass to Nam sooner or later."

Ken went back to Jacksonville and met up with family and friends. One of the young ladies he knew was Careva Woods. Norton didn't have much time for women while in basic or at Pensacola, so he asked Careva, a lifelong friend for a date.

"I was a young, virile and handsome dude and Careva wanted me. I needed to let loose and she fit the bill.

"She was a beautiful woman and I was a horny young guy home to let off some steam. That 'steam' ended up with Careva getting pregnant. I wasn't happy. I thought of what my mother went through and offered to marry Careva, but she turned me down. It was the right decision for both of us.

I was soon going to North Carolina to Camp Lejeune and it would be a burden for both of us. Also, I didn't know where I was going to end up. Probably Vietnam. Would it be fair for a young mother to be away from home in a strange place with a husband sent overseas? Careva made sense. With no one there to assist her—family, parents and friends? A marine's wife far from family and friends raising a young child and not knowing if her husband would ever return in one piece, if at all. Yeah, we all make mistakes, but I credit Careva for talking me out of marriage. She was smarter about those things than me. I actually have her to thank for not tying me down in Jacksonville. Ironically, a few years later, she married my cousin Gilbert and by that time our son, Keith Anthony was born. Today, he's a fine young man, working in Houston. Like me, he's a former Marine and I've grown close to him over the years. Keith was never bitter about the fact that I wasn't always there. Gilbert and Careva were the perfect match and I'm grateful to her for knocking some sense into me. I'm proud of Keith and his mother and my cousin Gilbert. Keith understood my situation and never, never uttered a disparaging word to me. In fact, we're closer now. It's never too late to be a father to a son and Keith and I appreciate each other. My cousin Gilbert and Careva are a happy couple and did a great job in bringing up Keith, just like my parents, Ruth and John Norton did for me. I have a lot to thank Careva."

Ken Norton reported to his post at Camp Lejeune, North Carolina and was immediately attracted to the football team. Informed that the best way to avoid getting up at 5AM for reveille was to perform in either football or boxing and get to tour the country. It would also be a good experience and probably avoid Vietnam duty. Norton, the football hero at Jacksonville decided to try out for the football team and ran immediately into trouble! But, he got to eat better food, not just the rations metered out to the privates. He would be in a special class and he knew he was up to the task.

"I wanted those extra perks and I knew I could excel at football and end up touring for the marines and avoid eating the same, bland rationed foods and possibly avoid getting my ass shot in Vietnam.

"I remember telling the coach that I wanted to try out for halfback. The halfback at the time was an officer who I knew I could outshine."

Norton knew that tension was in the air. He saw that the officer, a white redneck, looked at him with envy. He had seen that look before from other people growing up. He knew that this officer could pull rank and he was ready not to be a jerk but instead let his talents shine through. He would wait for the right time.

"He wouldn't look me in the eye, always diverting attention when I was around and tried to make me feel uncomfortable. I've been around people who had these limitations before, but he was an officer and I had to be careful. Very careful. He couldn't keep up with me and he knew it, but wasn't man enough to admit it. The coach didn't want to take sides but I knew a day of reckoning was near. I hated the fact that I had to put up with bullshit and not be myself."

Before long, a scuffle broke out with Norton and the white office used racially insensitive language after Ken tackled him and left him flat on the field. "He wasn't going anywhere after he was tackled by me. Besides, he deserved it—he deserved it.

"I heard the 'n' word used before but I just couldn't allow this idiot to get away with it. He was to blame. I walked off the field and coming into the locker room was met by Pappy

Dawson, an older ex-Marine now in charge of the boxing team. When he asked me why I left practice early, I explained that I was no longer wanted on the team. What he next suggested changed my life."

What Pappy Dawson suggested was for Norton to try boxing for the Marines.

Ken Norton's world was to change forever on that eventful day.

Chapter 7

"My dad, John Norton, used to watch the Friday night 'Gillette Cavalcade of Sports' on the old black and white TV set we had. I'd join him and saw Floyd Patterson knock out Ingemar Johannsen from the center of boxing in those days, New York City's Madison Square Garden." The old garden on 8th Avenue and 50th Streets. This was the place where Joe Louis beat Max Schelling, where Rocky Marciano fought and, before boxing headed west to Vegas, was the Mecca of the boxing world. It was also here in the late 1950's and early 1960's that much of America would watch 'the fights.' Pizza and beer parties brought families and friends together in countless bars and taverns across the US. Bets, some legal and some not, were won or lost depending on the outcome. Like most sporting venues in the then smoked-filled gritty taverns throughout America, arguments broke out as to who really was the better fighter, who delivered the best punches and was the boxer having an off night. So it was that the youngster from Jacksonville saw not only Patterson but also the ugly and tragic side when Emile Griffith knocked out Benny 'Kid' Paret in 1960 into a coma that he never came out of. That tragic event left a bitter taste in Ken Norton's mouth and he shied away from boxing, despite the fact that his father once remarked, "You have the size and speed to be a fighter."

"I really didn't think about it. I didn't want someone pounding my face—my good looks meant a lot to me. Call me vain, but I was always told I was good-looking and I didn't want to have a face that would turn off the women and worse, scar me with broken bones and a nose the size of Pinnochio!" Norton admits to being a control freak when it came to sports, be it football, track or basketball. He knew his sports, his ability and never thought of himself as a boxer.

"I was brought up in a stable household that frowned on violence and I knew I could knock off just about anyone but I didn't go looking for trouble and I avoided the rough and rowdy ones. I had a few scuffles in high school and people knew my temper and to stay away from me." Time changes a person's outlook and now it was another momentous change of events in the life of the young marine.

He was about to enter a strange world that would forever change his life as he knew it.

The old gentleman, Pappy Dawson, was tragically killed in a freak bus accident, just as Ken's training began. He took this to be an omen to persevere and not give up, despite his initial awkwardness in shadow boxing and sparing. Something told him to stay with the program. Norton made sure he was alone lest the other marines on the boxing team looked at him as a point of ridicule and a dilletante just out to avoid being in the mix of the rest of the marines. The boxing team, like the football team he left, had it perks when it came to better food and touring the country recruiting for others to sign up. It would be a means to an end and a possible career while avoiding being shipped overseas to an ever-increasing escalation of the Vietnam War. While in the gym, he looked around and made sure that others weren't there. He was, after all, new to this venue and didn't want to embarrass himself. But, ever the loyal and faithful son, he felt an attachment to the old man who just passed and was determined to give his all.

"Sometimes I'd wait until the other boxers left before I began my routine. The stench was bad. The place reeked of the familiar gym smell, but I was one not to give up and I was determined. I donned my trunks, laced up the shoes, put on the gloves and was ready." The young gladiator soon found that the routine—jumping rope, jogging, punching the bag, shadow boxing and finally sparing agreed with him. He was comfortable in his own skin, gaining the confidence and respect of both coach and fellow boxing marines. Others started noticing too.

What resulted was a three month trial that saw Ken Norton jogging more every morning, jumping rope longer and hitting the bag harder and harder. At first, he was just an upstart. But, after a few weeks, others in the gym saw a fierce, determined, strong and quick-learner. No longer apprehensive, he was ready to show his fellow marines that they had an opponent that was willing to give his all. What emerged from that rigorous three-month training, was a fighter. A formidable opponent ready to shine. He would look them straight in the eye and that cockiness that made him a star athlete in Jacksonville was again emerging.

Within a year, Ken Norton's agility in the ring was like the new star on Broadway.

He scored an impressive record of 10-1 in the Marine Corps. "I knocked out most of my opponents." The routine gave way to a trademark systematic, left-upper cut that few could withstand. Confident, eyeballing his opponent, he was in his venue and he knew it. He liked it and the power it gave him. So did others. Everyone wanted to witness for themselves the upstart marine from the Midwest. He became a topic of discussion, this time in the mess hall, clubs adjoining the base and the town surrounding it. Like a good Broadway show, his presence in the ring was theater of the highest form that played to an audience intent on seeing a spectacle that got notice. And people liked what they saw. Like a melodrama, the surprise, the action and the man came into being. Broadway at its best, only this time in the ring. A heavyweight boxer was born. The locals started calling him the "Golden Boy" because of the flashy, gold colored trunks he wore.

As with all new stars, he got noticed in the press. The Camp Lejeune News plastered his picture and gave him the respect he had back as a young dynamo in Jacksonville. Like in high school, people spoke to him, asked him where he was headed and started following his career.

Young, handsome, strong and virile he also got the attention from the females—lots of attention. Norton recalls that "a lot of girls stopped me to talk and flirt and I got to meet many, many women." One stood out among the others, though. She was a young, single mother named Jeanette. She was the one that didn't go chasing after him and he looked upon Jeanette as his challenge.

Jeanette Brinson was the 19 year old daughter of a night-club owner. She was a very slim, taciturn yet beautiful woman with perfectly manicured hair that completed her wholesome yet slim figure. She had no clue about the upstart boxer and didn't seem interested in him. What a challenge for Norton! Women always gave him a look and he wouldn't let this prize get away.

"She lived with her parents and her young son, Tommy. She finally started talking to me and we began dating. It wasn't long before I was in love with Jeanette and within a short time, she got pregnant. This time, I felt I was ready to make the commitment and marry her."

Norton married Jeanette, moving into an apartment on

the base at Camp Lejeune.

As fate would have it, Norton was transferred back to Pendleton. Wanting the best for his wife and yet unborn child, he asked her to move into his parents' home in Jacksonville, far away from the niche and comfort of her North Carolina roots.

For a pregnant, newly married 19 year old, this was a big change. Leaving her nest and going to live in far off Jacksonville, Illinois, a place as foreign as any to her. And scary. The change was too much and it showed as soon as she arrived at the home of Ruth and John Norton.

Ruth Norton recalls, "I tried to make conversation with her, make her feel at home and be part of our family. She was painfully shy to the point that others thought she was rude and reclusive. Things don't always work out well and this situation was bad all around. I felt for the girl, but she made it difficult by staying hours-on-end in her room and making little effort to converse." Indeed, Ruth would sometimes find Jeanette sitting silently, peering out the window at nothing in particular and it worried her that perhaps the wrong decision was made.

Alone, without Ken or her son Tommy, Jeanette's isolation didn't go unnoticed. The reclusive young wife tried to fit in but was an emotional wreck. Ruth and John and their extended family and friends accepted her as one of their own, but it was a difficult time. Yet, a healthy son named Kenneth Howard Norton Jr. came into the world on September 29, 1966.

"I was happy to have a son and although it took two months before I could see him, he was one fine young, healthy baby. I was happy as any new dad could be."

His son, the future Superbowl star of the Dallas

Cowboys and San Francisco 49ers was Ken's pride and joy the second he saw him at his parents' home.

Events were happening rapidly for Ken, his wife and son. Jeanette and Ken took their baby to North Carolina and to his surprise, Jeanette indicated that she would prefer to stay with her parents for a time.

"No doubt she missed her son Tommy and I could understand that. But, we were family now and I had to get back to base and resume my boxing with the marines in far off Pendleton. Frankly, I didn't want to miss my chances and stay stuck in North Carolina and end whatever fate had in store for me. Besides, I had to take orders from the marines and was told to go back to Pendleton. By this time, the Vietnam conflict had escalated and the call for more troops from the Pentagon was making life very stressful for us. I didn't know, despite my prospects as a boxer, if I was to be deployed to 'Nam."

Ken mentioned to Jeanette that she should join him soon after her visit with her parents. But he added: "I want to take Kenny with me to California." He had to. Norton didn't want to be without his young son.

What happened next was Jeanette agreeing to let her newly born son go with his dad to the other side of the country. This decision would have a major impact on their relationship.

"I should have realized that something wasn't kosher. She was quick to say 'ok' and didn't look me straight in the eye. I knew she missed her home and her parents. I guess I didn't realize the extent of it."

Instead of joining her husband within a few months, Jeanette stayed for six months, making Ken Norton a single father in charge of his infant son. A stressful time with war raging and a son to take care of and a career that was just getting noticed, Ken Norton was young, ambitious and anxious yet knew that he had to be a father to his son.

"I was back in San Diego. Yes, San Diego! The beautiful weather, the ocean, that alluring roar of the ocean, the warm sun shining down as I jogged along the beach. It was my niche. I felt at home but I got lonely—very lonely. I was a young buck, in my 20's. Women of all backgrounds would smile and give me that nod and I knew I could have my choice. I tried to stay faithful but I was alone with a baby to take care of, stressed to the max and yet I had my needs.

"Those beautiful California girls that the Beach Boys sang about were real and every day I ventured out I would see some and get aroused."

Women on the beach, in the stores, the clubs, the streets. "I couldn't avoid eye contact and would respond when they smiled back."

Ken Norton, like any young man, was in need. He was lonely. The women started to respond and he grew further and further apart from Jeanette. Days turned into weeks and weeks turned into months. Jeanette was not there and he needed company.

"I started dating a few ladies and was very honest about my situation. Some were turned off, but others had their own similar problems and were sympathetic. Once I started 'seeing' some ladies, it was hard to stop."

What Ken Norton experienced is the need to be in someone's company when a void exists. He knew he was cheating, but he couldn't help it. Jeanette wasn't there, despite his pleas for her to come home to him and their baby. Events are like that in life and it bonded Ken to his young son, Kenny even more.

"I'd look in the mirror sometimes and asked myself 'what the hell are you doing?'"

When Jeanette finally came out to San Diego, they both knew it was over. The absence made them grow apart and Jeanette indicated that she didn't want to stay away from her Carolina roots.

"Some of the females would call and I was always told to tell the truth. I did and it hurt, I know, but it was for the best.

"I didn't lie; I told her that there were others and she left. She loved Kenny, but didn't take him with her. As a single mother with a young son already, it would be difficult for her to raise two. The main reason I feel is that she knew by now that Kenny and I had grown close and I couldn't let go. Never!"

Ken Norton became the single father that anyone would be proud of. The parents that raised him instilled that strong bond and he wouldn't let Kenny go. They were family and needed each other.

Ken's career with the marines was drawing to a close. He didn't go to Vietnam and instead, as a single father in 1967, was given a chance to box and turn professional.

His honorable discharge behind him, he and his son headed to Los Angeles to train and try to make a life.

As he explained in his autobiography, *Going the Distance,* "San Diego was a beautiful city and I loved being by the ocean. But I had to make a living and the boxing gyms were in LA." So, he and his son packed up and moved up the coast to Los Angeles not knowing what was in the future.

Chapter 8

Single fathers don't get the attention, respect and accolades they deserve. Usually, it's the single mothers that get the attention. They have to provide and be a mother and look for work or try to get an education. Talk shows always portray a young, single mom with her kid while she struggles and holds down a job or goes to evening classes to complete an academic or trade curriculum. Responsible, dedicated, loving single moms deserve respect as they get up, make sure the child is up early, sent to the day care facility and get to their job. They deserve to get the attention and respect from a society that frowns upon a family devoid of a male figure. Rarely do single fathers get the attention and same respect. Dysfunctional perhaps in the traditional family setting, they are placed in an even more challenging situation. Being a mother and dad all rolled into one. Yet, not enough is said for the single father. His intentions are as solid and founded as any parent, and in many ways, even more demanding. Like the single mom, he has to provide for his child. He also has to get up early, making sure the child is fed and dressed for school or day care and begin his day traveling a distance to a job site with sometimes less than four hours of sleep. Across America, these are the unsung heroes. It was no different for a young father named Ken Norton. For Ken Norton and his young son, it meant moving to Los Angeles in the infamous Watts section that saw a few years earlier one of the most polarizing racial riots in American history, complete with National Guards. Norton had to leave the

tranquil, placid city of San Diego to be at a gritty, urban boxing gym, similar to the one that was featured in the
Philadelphia setting of 'Rocky.' The America of the late
1960's was rife with racial riots, calls for civil rights legislation to finally end the century old segregation and an end to
the unpopular and untenable war in Vietnam. The stress that
the nation endured was complemented by the upstart young
boxer, now living in a small, sparsely furnished apartment,
training daily at the nearby squalid yet receptive Hoover
Street Gym and trying desperately to make it on $100.00 a
week. Dreams of greatness, making it to the 'big time' don't
always materialize. Unknown numbers of aspiring boxers
throughout America have seen gyms like Hoover Street, gotten frustrated by not seeing instant results, packed up and
left. The quitters, those with attitudes who weren't giving
enough attention to their woman or just didn't 'get with the
program', became has beens, thrown to the mean and uncar-
ing street. Those willing to endure the endless and grueling
workouts had what it took to make it to the ring, be it amateur or professional. However, Ken Norton was one boxer
who knew exactly what he wanted from the Hoover Street
facility. He was the perfect candidate to be put under stress
and test his resolve. His determination, cockiness and ego-
driven talent that he knew were there had to be recognized.
He was ready to show anyone who he was, what he was capable of and there would be no turning back. But he had issues
and obstacles in the way. The fact that he had to be a responsible father, not some dead-beat who walked away from life's
hardships would make him ever stronger. "It toughened me
up and made me what I am today. Of all the titles that I've
been privileged to have, the title of 'dad' has always been the
best." For the moment, he had to deal with the old, rusty
gym that would make him a contender.

As Norton aptly explained: "To call it a gym by today's

standards is a stretch. It was a hole-in-the-wall place but it was where I learned my trade. The place reeked, it needed a painting, the lockers were old and in need of repair. Boxing may seem exciting and it was when seen on TV under the lights in a fancy Vegas arena. I can relate well to the poor, neighborhood kids who would come to get off the mean streets and strut their stuff and maybe, just maybe make it big time." The reality of the gym's fixtures—worn jump ropes hanging on a few broken hooks, several pair of well-worn boxing gloves, a ring with stains that told a history of countless young men who came looking for glory and ended up back on the mean streets of Watts, a few naked light bulbs hanging over the ring and an office to the side with a cluttered desk and a few faded posters of past gladiators. Yet, it was his niche, his place to shine and shine he would! Here in the gym is where legends were born and died and he was going to give 100% as always.

Ken Norton's life consisted of a very long day that involved getting up at the crack of dawn, running, jumping rope, sparing and taking his young son to his neighbors who babysat for him. Yet, the lack of money was real and soon he had to get a job at the Ford Motor Co., adding additional pressure to his dream.

"I had to drive to take Kenny to the babysitters and then get to the gym, get my workout started and go to Ford. I got home exhausted and yet had to be a father, mother and guardian all in one for my son. I learned not to let the routines of changing his diapers, cleaning and giving him attention get in the way. I welcomed it. He was my son. I was his contact, his father and I wanted to be there for him. In many ways, it made me tougher and appreciate the sacrifices that befall us." When he speaks of those difficult times, the gleam in his eyes is noticeable. This was the real test of manhood and he was there for Kenny first and foremost.

These lean years from 1967-1970 were tough ones for Ken and his young son. Shopping at the supermarket, buying baby food, diapers and coming home and washing his young son were all part of Ken Norton's life. Women would come and go. They would see the young son and soon panic and not want the responsibility of raising a kid that wasn't their own. Yet, like all his challenges, he was able to overcome. His son came first and no one would interfere in his biggest job—that of father. No one. He looks back on this part of his life and he realizes the strength he got from his parents, Aunt Mary and those people who believed in him.

Strength of character made Norton into a responsible father. He wouldn't have it any other way. His son was his life and no one would come between them, even if it meant giving up his dream of being a professional, forgoing dates with beautiful women or a night out. His steadfast resolve made him internally stronger and focused and prepared him not only for the ring but also for life itself. Others may have faltered and given up, but Ken Norton was no quitter. This trait, this gut instinct, this inner strength would certainly test him in the ring with the world looking on but it also got him though the even greater challenges following the freeway accident. He looked back on these years and attributes much of what he is today from the determination, fortitude and tests of those difficult years of the late 60's.

"I could have gone back to Jacksonville and been in a more comfortable situation. My mom would have helped raise Kenny and I was actually asked to break the color barrier by becoming the first black officer on the Jacksonville force. But, it was not for me. I was in my niche and I knew something would come of it. I was never a quitter and was not about to let these tough times win out. Not me, not me.

"Crazy as it may sound, that gym was my test and I wouldn't let it get the best of me. I would control the situation and leave any anger or attitude outside. The gym was my testing ground. It challenged me every day and, as I got more confident, I knew it was just a matter of time. My managers and sparing partners and even the lone maintenance man saw it too. It just gave me that extra incentive to get on with it."

Ken's devotion to his son and his unconditional love made him all the more stronger both in mind and body. He was determined more than ever to achieve not only for himself but also for Ken Jr. He had come to terms with himself, knowing that the grueling schedule and the attention needed by his son would, in the end, pay off. It was a lesson in human relations, in family bonding and the need to be wanted and be of service to someone else. These are the values that his parents expected and he was an ever bigger champion outside the ring—in the ring of life! Coping with the stress of being a single father, a provider, a worker and an aspiring world class boxer would have depleted many others. But this was Ken Norton, a fighter inside and out. No one would stop him from attaining his dream. The tough marine had the drive, the motivation, the 'gut' to get a job done. He was more steadfast, quicker on his feet, more aggressive in his sparing and it got noticed. But, above all, he was a dad to his boy and he would let no one stand in the way of that great bond. Courage comes in many facets and Norton had the whole package.

Norton's dream would eventually be fulfilled. Working long hours, taking time out for Ken Jr. and keeping his goals on target finally allowed him to make his debut as a pro in late 1967. He won his first fight, knocking out his opponent, Grady Brazell, in the third round. By early 1968, he had three wins and was on his way. He had a trainer, Eddie Futch, who believed in him, and by 1970, Norton had a record of 16-0 wins!

Despite the wins, Ken Norton still was having a rough time financially. Money is hard to come by for aspiring talents be it actors, dancers, writers or boxers. Fighters didn't make much unless there was a big event. He would get upset at times and wonder if he should give up and then, looking at his now four year old, he knew the efforts would pay off. At times, he thought of giving up, moving back with Kenny and getting a job in Jacksonville. He knew Kenny would ask about his mom and he would tell him that she just couldn't be there, but loved him. But, that same year, his self-assurance got in the way and he lost his first fight. Not used to losing, he eventually was introduced to a book by a hypnotist named Dr. Michael Dean. His trainer Eddie was concerned that the loss to a Venezuelan boxer named Garcia would sidetrack him and give him an excuse to cut loose. Eddie, however, knew Ken had what it takes to make it. Going to Dr. Dean made a difference and the book he suggested became his boxing bible. That book was Napoleon Hill's, *Think and Grow Rich*. Norton explains that the advice given in the book made him come to terms with himself.

"After winning 16 bouts and still feeling that I wasn't getting my due, working out and still having to hold down a job and raise Ken, I felt something was owed me. I was cocky, my trainer Eddie admitted as much and I needed perhaps the loss in 1970 to a boxer named Jose Luis Garcia to wake me up. He did just that! I needed to chill out! But the book by Hill became my Bible for survival. It was Dr. Phil, Oprah and Dale Carnegie all rolled into one. I especially liked and repeated 'The only man who wins is the one who thinks he can.' That was it."

The advice outlined in Hill's book became his mantra. He read the book over and over as if to convince himself he could do it. Events did take a drastic turn for the young pugilist and his talent was finally getting recognized.

What the world knows about Ken Norton is he is the fighter and the man who eventually triumphed over the Greatest, Mohammed Ali.

Norton started fighting more. By 1972, he had seven more wins under his belt and was finally making the money that allowed him to leave Ford and devote his energy, time and effort to the sport that was now his for the asking. He had been sparing with Joe Frazier and felt he had arrived.

"Joe Frazier paid me $500.00 a week to spar with him. I earned every penny of it."

Frazier was a tough fighter who hit hard and helped Norton on his way. The daily routine of sparing coupled with the exercises eventually caught the eyes of promoters and by 1973 Ken Norton was ready to face the greatest fighter of his generation, Muhammad Ali. That happened on March 31, 1973, when the world was stunned by the defeat of Ali by Ken Norton. Overnight, the sports world took notice and Ken Norton was no longer the struggling stay-at-home dad but was now the North American Boxing Federation belt holder—a champion. The fight, broadcast on national television from the San Diego Sports Arena, caught Ali by surprise. As Ali later admitted: "I didn't train adequately for the match and had trouble avoiding Norton's quick advances." Norton, always very focused, was in top form mentally and physically. He broke Ali's jaw in the first round.

In a 12 round decision, the fight was given to Norton. It was just the second fight that the Greatest lost. Ali recalled that Norton was one tough fighter and in each of the three fights with Ali, the decision was always close and controversial.

Fame has its rewards but Ken Norton, now an overnight sensation that stunned the boxing world, was the man of the hour.

"I managed to shut up the motor machine of Ali. I felt bad that his jaw was broken but it was just one of the awful things that come along with the rough sport. No one likes to see someone hurt, but everyone wanted to know the man who shut up Ali!"

When Norton would venture out, he was greeted by people who, days earlier, didn't know who he was or took notice. Fame affects people in strange ways, but thanks to Norton's upbringing and his resolve to provide for Ken Jr. and persevere, it paid off not only financially but also professionally. Calls came in to his manager and trainers and the purse increased as did the offers.

"Calls came in, I got noticed, my picture was on every sports page in *Boxing News, Sports Illustrated* and people like Howard Cosell gave me national coverage.

"Johnny Carson's people called and I was the guest on his 'Tonight Show.' I was nervous at first on the show, but felt at ease when Carson started joking that I was the only person in America who could shut up Ali.

"Yes, I was written up in all sports papers and magazines, was interviewed on national TV and yet, I didn't let it go to my head. Just a few months later, I lost to Ali in a 12 round rematch in Los Angeles. Another split decision. And, yeah, the women were there, but by now, I had met and married Jackie and was settled." Jackie was a single mother with a son named Brandon and before long, Norton was married for the second time. "We had a small ceremony and settled in Los Angeles County." Eventually, a daughter would be born to Jackie and Ken named Kenisha. Born in 1976, she was naturally spoiled by her doting father. A son, Ken E. Jon also came along a few years later. Loving the sun and the ocean and beach, the now famous pugilist was seen on the beach in LA County jogging alone or with his wife and children. It wasn't until three years after his accident that he moved to suburban Orange County in Southern California, where he resides to this day.

Gone were the long, hard days that saw Norton first and foremost a father to Kenny, putting off vacations and dinner dates. His son was his biggest priority and he, the single father would be cited years later as the twice-won 'Father of the Year.' He knew in his heart he was giving his all to his son. That's all that mattered. Courage comes in many forms. Picture the first year teacher in a difficult urban school, the new enlistees now serving in Iraq not knowing their fate, the single mother waiting on tables whose husband abandoned her and left her to make it alone, the politician who actually tells the truth despite the consequences at the polls or the cop who doesn't turn his head at witnessing brutality by his fellow officer and turns him in. This form of courage goes largely unnoticed but later the rewards are there and the results show a sense of fair play, a desire to get the job done well, a moral conviction to right a wrong. Norton's unwavering attention to his young son and still seeking his dream of making it in the ring was largely unnoticed by the press. Had stories been printed about the sacrifices he made to ensure that his son was fed and the long, grueling hours spent working at the plant and perfecting his skills at the Hoover Street Gym, the unassuming Norton would have grabbed the attention of the literary world with a real feel-good story. Movies could have shown him as the real come from-behind

kid who made it. For Ken Norton, boxer and father represented the best that is in all of us—a person who had his
misfortunes and share of setbacks yet never gave up. Yet the
most important person he won over was himself. Even if he
had lost to Ali in the first of what was to be three bouts with
the Greatest, he had proven to his trainers and his manager
that he had the guts and stamina to believe in himself.
Fighting Ali or any other boxer was no ordinary event, no
ordinary sports' night, no Friday night at the old Madison
Square Garden. Boxing had become theater, replete with
fanfare, worldwide coverage via satellite TV, celebrities, adoring fans and greedy bettors. What a spectacle! Not unlike its
origins in the ancient Colosseum of Rome. Like the ancient
Romans, spectators were there for the kill and expected
drama of the highest form. They were hungry and wanted to
be entertained. They liked surprises and a topic to discuss
over cocktails. Unlike a Broadway show, this was unscripted
and unrehearsed, each round unique, forcing the boxer to
constantly change his script accordingly. Like the actors on
stage, they had to perform and win over the audience. Yet,
these were special actors. Like thousands before them in the
ring, they had the power to perfect their craft, rewrite the
script as it evolved and show them what made them unique.
All the preparation, all the long hours, the special diets, the
abandonment of pleasures and late night forays were aimed
at this event. The arenas became for them not just a meal
ticket but their starring role as great as on the Hollywood
screen itself.

Norton likes to mention that he has the greatest respect
for Ali and in two subsequent bouts, lost to the Greatest. He
smiles when he's reminded of that famous first bout and
remembers the great entourage Ali brought with him. He
recalls that 30 people surrounded him while he had his manager, trainer and a few friends escort him to the ring near San

Diego. He was the underdog and knew that all the braggadocio and hoopla that made Ali so enduring to many, made Ken all the more determined to show the world that he was ready." I think he had a custom pair of trunks that Elvis sent him." And ready he was!

The outcome of the fight is one for the history books, with the jaw of Ali broken, turning the boxing world on its heels. The motormouth Ali was now rendered speechless and Norton became the man of the hour. Yes, gone were the blank stares from people who didn't recognize him.

"Before the Ali fight, few people recognized me. After it, I was greeted on the street, in the mall, restaurants, on the golf course and asked to sign autographs, have pictures taken by anyone with a camera and given the eye by many females."

Over the next eight years, Norton made boxing his life. With his quick jabs and strong frame and one, two punch combination he amassed an impressive record of 42 wins, 7 losses and one tie. Legendary fighters from the Golden Age of Boxing during the 1970's and 1980's included the likes of: Charlie Reno, George Foreman, Jerry Quarry, Duane Bobick, Jimmy Young, Larry Holmes, Earnie Shavers, and Gerry Cooney. Places as diverse as San Diego, New York City, Caracas, Venezuela; San Antonio, and Landover, Maryland were all places where Norton fought.

"I remember the 1976 third fight with Ali. The promoters wanted a venue that would attract a lot of people and they chose Yankee Stadium in the Bronx. The place was absolute chaos, as the police were having a slowdown with City Hall and the people just jammed the streets with little or no organization and no police protection. In some cases, crowds even turned over cars and hordes of youngsters frightened even veteran and seasoned New Yorkers." The venue at the stadium was chaotic with many young people shouting 'Ali, Ali.' This was the South Bronx of then burned-out buildings, open drug dealing, graffiti-laden subway cars replete with 'art' messages, broken windows and commuters who stared straight ahead and wished only to get their destination undeterred. But there were dreamers in that crowd of 30,296 fans. One of them, Alex Ramos, a South Bronx resident, wanted desperately to see the fight. He and a group of his friends snuck into the stadium, having been to Yankee games before and knowing the secret yet clandestine hidden passages. Seeing such a seminal event would transform young Ramos into a wannabe fighter after seeing Norton, his idol, fight. "Ken left a great impression on me. I knew I wanted to be part of this action." But the madness in the street gave way to theater in the ring. It was no surprise that arriving guests at the stadium were intimidated by the rowdy, loud and menacing crowds of youngsters, knowing the police slowdown would only give them an added sense of control. Ken Norton was there to fight. Aware of the street events, his focus was entirely on the fight and his formidable opponent in the ring.

Most of his boxing career was not marred by a circus atmosphere outside the arena or stadium. Ken Norton was now used to the fanfare and the applause and the attention but it didn't ever get to him or remake him into a high profile sought after idol. "I went to Studio 54 and saw all the crowds downstairs dancing and upstairs in the VIP lounge. I just didn't take all the glory seriously. I had women swooning over me and people all around taking pictures and 'hi-five' and it was fun. I was the hot item, the new kid on the block and the New York crowd loved Ali but respected me. That's the way I liked it, complete with my head held high." Ken Norton had a job to do and, as he learned from his parents, he gave it his all. Thus, Norton performed his job well, paying little or no attention to the crowds, both in and out of the stadiums, arenas and nightclubs, focusing entirely on his career. Yes, it was a fun ride. Yet the final fight with Ali at Yankee Stadium was something no one could forget.

By 1977, the 34 year old Norton was given the Fighter of the Year Award after knocking out Duane Bobick. He was at the pinnacle of his career.

Although the 1976 fight at the stadium resulted in an Ali victory, it lasted the full 15 rounds and Norton and many of the sports writers and officials felt that Norton had actually won. Norton, ever the gentleman, didn't dwell on it. He continued his quest and continued to fight up to 1981, his last event with George Cooney. To this day, his record of 42 wins and 7 losses and one draw is an impressive one of which he is justly proud. It also gave him fame, money and a new career, later as a screen idol, appearing in movies, beginning in 1975 with *Mandingo*, followed by *Drum* a year later.

Millions of fans were thus drawn to the muscular, handsome and alluring man who had defeated Ali. Jokingly, he said: "They picked me because DeLaurentis, in filming *Mandingo*, wanted someone hot and in the spotlight. Also, I was better looking than Ali, Foreman and Frazier!" Although canned by the critics, the role of the slave Mede in a steamy, interracial sexual encounter with the lead made Ken Norton much in demand on the big screen. The movie, based on a popular novel by Kyle Onstott made Norton a star. He had appeal by virtue of his looks, physique and on screen presence. Acting became a job for him and he tackled it head on. Like all encounters, he faced his acting debut and made a favorable impression on the director and producer. He also got to act with such Hollywood notables as James Mason, Brenda Sykes, Susan George and Richard Ward. Like the focused boxer he was, he plunged into his roles and made every effort to excel, working with an acting coach along the way. "All those takes to get it just right. Even the steamy sexual encounter had to be done over and over. It was a job!" After filming *Mandingo*, offers started to come in for the handsome, rugged Norton. He continued his acting lessons and, like every good student immersed himself into the dynamic of technique, speech and delivery. Ever focused, he got better and the demand got greater and the offers came in for the rugged boxer. He was hot and Hollywood was ready for him. In all, he made over 20 movies beginning with *Mandingo*, followed by *Drum* in 1976, to the role of Jackhammer in *A-Team* in 1983 with Mr. T., to the not so acclaimed features as the 1985 *Cover-Up Black Widow*. His post-accident life didn't deter him from the allure of the screen and in the 1990's he appeared as a security guard in *Frog and Wombat* and as himself in 1998 in *Dirty Work*. He still managed to appear on TV specials, such as The Arsenio Hall Show and in 2004 was again cast as himself in the production *The Next Great Champ*. Hollywood, both pre—and post-accident, liked the ease and swagger of Ken Norton and the audience responded in kind.

Chapter 9

By the time of that fateful night of February 22, 1986, Ken Norton was a man who had it all. Fame, fortune, family and now a son Ken Jr. who was a star athlete just as he was in his native Jacksonville. A soon-to-be graduate of UCLA, Ken Norton Jr. would earn a BA degree in sociology. During his four years at college, young Norton had packed a solid 254 lbs and was the star linebacker for the UCLA Bruins. Like his famous father, he was the star on the football college circuit and the subject of talk. It was no secret that he had his eyes on the pros and the college scouts were soon showing up and the talks began. It was at this time, as he was nearing the end of his college days, when his hero dad suffered the freeway accident.

Tragedies affect people in many ways. Some despair, giving up the fight and allowing the injuries they sustained to overwhelm them, sending them into a long and tragic depression. Others, family members, give up their time and effort to provide for a loved one. Especially today, as parents age, many middle-aged children find themselves looking for assisted living for an elderly parent while maintaining dignity and allowing them to remain in their own homes. Much the same happens when a family member, young or old, suffers long-term injury and is in need of 24 hour care.

Coming home, Ken Norton had family members there for him. His son, the one he never abandoned and raised single-handedly would not allow his dad to give up. About to begin a stellar career that would see him in the NFL, his first concern was his dad. Ken Norton Jr. did for his dad what his dad did for him two decades before—perform the daily necessary tasks so needed by someone in Ken Norton's position. Like the prodigal son, he returned to the nest and was ready for his dad.

Ken Norton was justifiably proud of his son. This period in his rehabilitation would make him all the more proud. He had raised him while struggling to get his boxing career started. Now, a star athlete in football, just like his dad before him, Ken Jr. was on his way.

"He could have walked away, using the excuse that his career was taking off and that I could afford a 24 hour nurse. It's true, but my son wouldn't stand for that. He knew that, as a man, I would need someone there for me 24/7."

Events were going well for Norton, his wife, sons and daughter. Then the unexpected happened on that February night. It changed everything.

In a complete reversal 20 years later, the son became the care-giver for the father. Fate does strange things. Uncontrollable events test our strength of character. Events, such as the one that occurred off the freeway ramp, forever changed Ken Norton's life. But, events are not isolated to the person affected. They impact upon the rest of the family and friends. This would be a situation that was most challenging to anyone, especially testing the resolve of a talented, young versatile athlete. The father who had reared him, taught him the necessary manners and right from wrong. The father who was there for him while he struggled to make it in the boxing world, working two jobs yet never forgetting his first priority to his young namesake.

"I knew Dad would need care and I wanted to be there

for him as he was for me." As soon as he learned of the freeway accident, he was at his bedside. What he saw made him reevaluate life. Ken Jr. remained with his father despite his now own grueling schedule of college and football.

"Dad was like a train wreck. Depressed, angry and moody, I knew it would be a real challenge to make sure he came around." Ken Jr., like his father, was also a focused, stubborn person who wouldn't allow circumstances to overwhelm him. "He wanted so desperately to get well as fast as possible, but knew it would take time." His boxing regimen helped him come to terms with the slow but steady progress. The challenges he faced to get to the professional boxing world paled in comparison to this struggle. Yet, he wouldn't give in and once his mind was made up, he set his goal to walk and eventually drive his own car.

"Coming home was difficult. I was determined to get to all the therapy sessions which included vocal and physical. My son dressed me, cleaned me, drove me to the sessions and helped get me back on track. I wish I could have spoken to him. It was difficult with the vocal cords damaged and I practiced often before a mirror, trying to get the words out. This was the major challenge for me."

Nights were difficult too. Like most recovery victims, pain was a constant and a mere four or five hours of sleep was all he could gather. His right leg—the one that had been nearly crushed in the accident, wouldn't respond and remained stiff and painful for the next two years. It ached constantly despite the painkillers. His skull was nearly crushed and he insisted on wearing a hat to cover up the scars that the accident left as a permanent reminder. He used to love to walk along the beach and hear the roar of the ocean and the surf and feel the breeze of a fresh, new day while glancing at the sky and seeing the gulls and assorted birds fly by. Now, it was so different, so very different. He was an invalid in need and young Ken made the decision that his dad had to come first.

Young Ken had to carry his father to and from the bathroom and be a constant friend and confidant as well. "It's hard to come to terms with life-altering experiences for anyone and more difficult for an active and responsive person like Dad." Lifting his dad so he could perform the necessary functions of bathing, cleaning and dressing was no small task, even for the soon to be NFL athlete. Like the prodigal son, he learned to return what had been done for him years earlier. Times of trauma and uncertainty make or break a family or relationship. The true bond that had been established by Ken Norton barely getting by and yet providing for his son was now put to the test. Despite his stressful life of college and football, young Ken far exceeded where others might falter.

"I'm glad I was able to carry dad." At 254 lbs of solid muscle, he was up to the task and was there for his dad. More importantly, as with every person in need, he listened to his father and gave him the encouragement to move on. Instead of staring at the steps, he made it a focal point in his quest for recovery. "Those 14 steps became the challenge, like a boxer stepping into the ring to face his opponent. Not knowing what to expect, you gave it your all." 14 steps seemed like an impossible mission, but it was one that gave Norton the incentive to move and persevere.

Ken Norton's recovery, like any victim suffering permanent injuries, had to first face reality and then make the adjustments incrementally towards recovery. His survival was as much mental as physical and the reality check that was thrust upon him had to be dealt with head-on.

Ken's resolve wouldn't waver and his determination accelerated the healing process. He had a new lease on life. Special occasions, such as a birthday, anniversary or holidays from Thanksgiving, Christmas and Easter started to have a new meaning.

"Everything changed after the accident. My life was never going to be the same, but I wasn't going to give up. Sure, I had days that I just sat in the wheelchair and stared at the window but I got over that. I was too strong mentally to let the demons take over and dictate my life. I was taught to believe in yourself and treat people the way you wanted to be treated. I soon learned that family was there and Ken Jr. in particular."

Young Ken knew that his father would be tough and yet he was as determined as he to accelerate the recovery process. Going to appointments, conducting the oral and physical exercises outlined by the therapist are part of any patient's path to recovery. What made it all the more important for young Ken was the special patient, his dad. Ken recalls in the 2000 biography, *Going the Distance*,: "Dad didn't know what happened to him. The events of the accident were blurred. At times, he would tell me that he wanted to drive and I knew he couldn't yet. He was stubborn, but that same stubborn attitude actually helped him recover faster. I think that same stubbornness ultimately got him out of that wheelchair."

Indeed, Ken Norton wanted to walk and take the handicapped sticker off the windshield of the car. He remained in the wheelchair for a long two years while the physical therapist, Dr. Janice Kowalski evaluated his progress. Her famous patient was one that wouldn't take no for an answer and the painful, repetitious exercises finally paid off. Progress can be measured in stages. The physical regimen included: lifting light weights to get the muscles strengthened, acupuncture and swimming. Physical rehabilitation can see results if the patient is mentally ready and the famous patient was very eager and always prepared to meet the challenge. With the help of his son Ken, Norton's stubbornness paid off. He not only religiously adhered to Dr. Kowalski's therapy but also showed progress by getting from a wheelchair into a walker.

"I would stare at those damn 14 steps leading up to the second floor bedroom. I looked upon those steps as I did an opponent in the ring. I would rise, holding onto the walker and take a step. Ken Jr. would always guide my step and within the first year I was able to make it up a few steps. That's what progress is all about."

Progress to a person who had it all now meant a day-to-day existence of dependency on those who were there. The twist of fate that now had the elder Norton being cared for by the young Ken was a tribute to Ken Norton's determination as a young single father to make time for his son. Now, with the tables reversed, it was the son who became the hero. Ken Jr. assisted his father by taking the time to be there—to help him initially get to the bathroom, wash him, clothe him and make sure that his medication was taken, his therapy appointments met and also acted as his agent whenever anyone of note or family called. But, progress was made and day by day the depression lifted a bit and a smile came across his face. The headsets were there for him to listen to jazz and the melodic tones of Sarah Vaughn, Ella Fitzgerald, Luther Vandross, Sinatra and occasionally pop groups from the Spinners to the Commodores.

"With the music and his plaques, belt and trophies nearby, dad was coming around," Ken Jr. recalls. So much of a person's pace depends upon attitude. Ken Norton was one who had the positives—the attitude was not only positive but also one of determination to persevere and get up from the wheelchair and onto the walker and walk unassisted. His goals were at once simple yet complex but, like the fighter he was, no one was going to tell him otherwise.

"I know he was in pain trying day after day to rise from that wheelchair, but I couldn't stop him. His face would tighten, he would grip the arms of the chair with his powerful arms and stand as straight as he could. He never held back and never complained. His mantra now became: 'I can lick this. Just watch and you'll see.'"

Ken Jr. went on to explain: "When he first looked into the mirror, he was looking down and not straight. Like some school boy in the principal's office being reprimanded, he had a sad, almost distant look. That soon changed when he started to make progress getting out of the wheelchair. The smile returned, the face looked squarely into the mirror and the dad I knew was returning." The long hours of therapy coupled with a lot of love from family and especially Ken Jr. were the perfect remedy. The adjustments were made and I knew that those long, agonizing hours and words of encouragement were finally paying off."

Young Ken Norton sacrificed much for the man who had done so much to rear him and make him into a positive star athlete destined for the pros. All the time he spent with his dad, whether cleaning, feeding, entertaining or just talking with him paid off. Slowly, both men advanced. Ken Sr. started taking a few steps up those mighty 14 steps to the second floor bedrooms. No longer did Ken Norton feel any pity or ask "Why me?" He was eager to walk, go outside, drive his car and be part of the community again. Thanks to the efforts of his soon-to-graduate son, he was making great progress.

"Seeing him make those 14 steps was like hitting the lotto. It was his goal. He did it in two years. I don't think anyone but my dad could fess up to this, as he would nag us day after day to mentally record his progress. Like a young school kid, he was making the grade and he wanted to reach the summit."

The 14 steps were, for Ken Norton, like climbing Mt. Everest. It was an achievement he set out to conquer. And conquer it, he did.

"Once the first step was reached, it was an event that gave dad the incentive to continue and never give up. The carpeted stairway leading to the second floor landing had pictures on the wall with a chandelier hanging over the center. As he started his slow, steady climb, he'd look up at the chandelier measuring his progress or looking at the adjacent photos of us kids on the wall. It was very emotional yet a beautiful thing."

Once his father was walking and started to swim, he wanted to drive. The younger Ken reports that at first he would deliberately park his car behind his dad's van to stop him from trying to get behind the wheel.

"I knew he was stubborn. Once he started making progress both physically and mentally, I knew he would make it." Things wouldn't be the same, but at least he could walk albeit with a pronounced limp. His steps would be more deliberate and unsteady, but he continued to show major progress and was using a cane. The cane became his friend. Like a reliable friend, the cane was there. At first, he gripped it hard and was unsteady in his gait. Slowly, with a few steps, then a few more and finally walking the length of the room, progress was made and the smile started returning to his face. Soon a new cane appeared, complete with a gold top showing a golden lion. The golden lion atop the cane became symbolic of the transformation of the once mercurial, stubborn man into an eager, fast learner, intent on getting on with his life. Progress continued with Ken Jr.'s help. Once he could walk, it would only be a matter of time before he would drive. Indeed, Ken Norton was able to drive, joined a gym at Dana Point and began lifting weights to give him more strength and coordination. The personal trainer assigned to him had dealt with clients in rehabilitative states from car injuries or recovering from surgery. Ken's progress at the gym amazed his trainer who started to add a few more pounds with every session. The results started to show. As with most fitness centers, the Dana Point facility had mirrors surrounding the weight room to measure one's progress. Others in the gym gave additional encouragement and soon his strength returned. Coupled with the nutritional drinks and stretching and power point massages, he began to walk steadier, hold himself more erect and look into the mirror with a sense of pride. His once impressive physique started to firm up and although his limp remained and speech was slurred, his determination was there and he became his old self again. He ate better, looked at TV less, drove to see friends and managed to follow the meteoric rise of his son to the NFL. No longer angry, self-absorbed or contemplative, he instead became his son's biggest fan and followed his progress at UCLA and on to the NFL.

Ken Norton Jr. was drafted by the Dallas Cowboys. A linebacker, he would stay with the Cowboys from 1988-1993 before joining the San Francisco 49er's in 1994. His professional career was highlighted by his participation in Superbowl XVII which resulted in a Dallas victory and Superbowl XVIII. Recovering a fumble for Dallas, Ken Norton Jr.'s effort resulted in a winning touchdown which brought a superbowl win and the Lombardi Award. Likewise, from 1994-2000, Norton distinguished himself with the 49ers and ended up in the Superbowl once again. His #51 jersey was seen on TV and in person by his proud father. The large framed Norton towered above many of his teammates at 6'1." He still packed a solid 250lbs. A tackle by Norton meant only one thing—you were going down! Like a chess game, he was formidable as a defensive lineman and on offense, recovering fumbles and getting both the Cowboys and 49er's to the playoffs. His father had much to be proud of the son he raised. Young Norton's career, which ended in the NFL in 2000, saw an impressive array of statistics: 12 sacks, 5 interceptions and 13 fumbles recovered. Today, he is a proud parent residing in the Los Angeles area and the linebacker coach of the UCLA Trojans. Ken Norton Jr., the young son who was reared by his father during financially-challenged times was now as famous as his dad. Ken Jr., along with Deion Sanders, won consecutive superbowls on different teams. They are the only two professional football players to hold such a record.

Because of the damage to his vocal cords, it was difficult for Ken Norton to fully explain to the horde of reporters at the superbowls how he felt. Yet the smile on his face and the gleam in his eyes spoke volumes. Young Ken had come through. To see his son on the field excelling and making his mark was the perfect panacea on his road to recovery.

"I tried to express my feelings of pride when the reporters spotted me, but the words couldn't come out." Yet, anyone within sight of Ken Norton, knew the former boxer was now a recovering accident victim who witnessed the most-watched American sporting event. No doubt he reflected on the meager years when he was living day to day and trying to raise young Ken with the same solid values his parents had for him.

Chapter 10

By 1998, twelve years after his near-fatal crash, Ken Norton was a 55 year-old survivor. A survivor who had exceeded beyond expectations in his recovery, amazing both the medical profession and his family. Able to drive on his own, he was often seen in the Dana Point community of Orange County in Southern California parking his Mercedes in the same favorite spot under the tree to protect his prized possession from the hot sun. He was indeed a survivor.

The former heavyweight champ had come to terms with his limitations, accepting them much like a battled combat soldier and moving on with his life. It wasn't easy, but he was able to cope. Life can be like that at times. Either we accept the consequences of a conflict, deal with it and move on or brood and allow the internal demons to take over. Capitulation was not a word in the Norton vocabulary. By now, his 'step didn't have as much pep,' due to the injuries to his right side. He was used to challenges in the ring and, like most boxers, was light on his feet. Now it was different. His right leg, damaged by the accident, gave way to a permanent limp. Yet, he was determined as ever to overcome and show the world and himself that this was no quitter. Less dependent and more self-assured, his hat ever atop his head, the proud, tall ex-boxer with the infectious grin would be in demand at the venues that line the coast, from the gym to the golf course to the restaurants to the jazz and dance clubs.

Always offering a smile whenever anyone recognized him, he was grateful for the attention he had earned so well. He was also grateful to be alive and see his son sparkle on the gridiron. And he was a proud dad. A very proud dad. His son, Ken Jr., now a star athlete in the NFL, gave Norton more reason to gloat on his offspring's accomplishments with the Dallas Cowboys and later the San Francisco 49er's. His heart swelled inside knowing that he had reared a son who was destined for sports history like himself. "He was going to make it big," he told anyone within earshot. He was at once recognizable and always approachable to the many fans who remembered him and those glorious days in the ring. A loyal fan would never be turned down for an autograph or picture. Always approachable, he was comfortable in his own skin. He had endured so much and had been through the agony of readjustment, accepting his fate and moving on. A person who knew pain both inside the ring and now outside, he became a role model to the many, yet often neglected survivors of catastrophic injuries. Ken Norton, the survivor, had come to terms with himself and knew that each day was a gift. The hometown values he learned so well from his parents and Aunt Mary sustained him. Never a quitter or complainer, he moved on and let the chips fall where they may. He had become larger than life as an athlete and now, in the most critical phase of his rehabilitation, he had proven to the rest of the world that the fighter instinct was there and no one could extinguish it. Yet, not all was rosy and cheerful. Events do happen and they happened to Ken Norton in swift progression.

The past decade was a tumultuous one for Ken Norton. It was during this period that his marriage to Jackie came unraveled. Good events and bad events are part of life. His marriage was coming apart and he knew it was just a matter of time."We just grew further and further apart. It wasn't the same and we both knew it," he remembers. Yet, he had his children. The proud father doted on his children. They were his life. His two children by Jackie, Kenisha and Ken Jon were a great source of pride as was his now famous son, Ken Jr. He was the doting father to his daughter, ever cautious of her whereabouts and warning any serious would-be suitor that he would be in their face and subject to the 'Norton Treatment.' Protective, suspicious yet knowing that she too would leave the nest for college and beyond, he often sized up her boyfriends, showing his still powerful fist in a gesture that was at once both comical and yet, a warning. Kenisha was his only daughter and Ken was the vigilant, cautious type who always screened her boyfriends to the point that she feared all would be driven away. It was part of his psyche, a product of his Midwest upbringing and he wouldn't let it go. But it was with the best of intentions for Kenisha and she was on her way to a successful career. The same could not be said of his relationship with his wife, Jackie. The marriage wasn't faring well and he would brood over it. The house had changed and so had both he and Jackie. Knowing that he was headed for a separation and eventual divorce, his forays to restaurants and clubs became more frequent. He needed an outlet and soon he found someone who would enter his life and make him whole again. Her name was Rose Marie Conant.

"Before Rose, I wasn't myself. I was moody. I would just sit there, looking at the trophies and the clippings scattered about and the photo shoots from the movies I was in. I'd think of the past and feel depressed. This was before Rose. She changed everything."

It takes someone special to make a change. Change in attitude, in perspective, in overall life itself. Feeling left out and lonely was not like Ken Norton and he needed an avenue to escape from the past. He had come to terms now with his challenges and handled the changes head on. Yet there was something missing. It wasn't just Jackie's absence, the kids growing up and needing space. It was his inner self trying to come to terms with his own mortality and he wanted to make the years ahead productive, creative and be a part of the world again. With the entry of Rose Marie Conant, that world changed over night.

Rose Marie Conant was a native Californian of Creole descent. Her roots were in Louisiana in the area of Cane River, Louisiana, an historic parish in the Northeastern and North central part of the state not far from Alexandria. The Cane River, as described on its tourist website, is "part of Natchitoches Parish, the oldest permanent settlement in the Louisiana Purchase." The Louisiana Purchase had doubled the size of the young republic in 1803 with the acquisition from the French dictator, Napoleon by Thomas Jefferson. Extending some 35 miles, the Parish was the site of antebellum slave plantations that aligned the shore of the river. Today it boasts a national historic park. On both sides of the windy river are found native Louisiana irises in shades of yellow and blue. Today, the flora and fauna of the area entice ecologists and other environmental studies examining the habitat of the many species along its riverbank. Thus, turtles, ducks, egrets and heron are common sights along the river. Imagine an explorer or a first-time visitor, oaring down the quiet riverbank and witnessing the rich, natural habitat. With a history as rich as the soil itself, the multicultural society of French, Spanish, Africans, Natchitoches Indians and Creoles made this part of Louisiana one of the most racially mixed areas of the United States. From its Indian roots to the French, Spanish and later Americans of both black slaves and freemen and white American settlers, it became a melting pot rich in the culture of its inhabitants. Rose Conant grew up, however, in California, attending the local parochial school, St Anselm's, and after finishing high school in Cerritos worked for Ford Aerospace and Communication Corporation for 13 years, obtaining a degree in accounting. Settling in Orange County, the young divorcee was a dedicated mother of two—Fabian and Chelsea. With her degree in accounting, she devoted her time and energy to her children. Like Ken Norton's early years as a single father, she was responsible for herself and the raising of her two children. No easy task for anyone. Like most young, now single people, she felt a void in her life. For a brief spell, she visited her native Louisiana, only to return to the Golden State. So she again looked west and headed back to familiar territory —California. Lured back to the seductive climate and nearby ocean, she resettled in Orange County with her daughter, Chelsea and son Fabian by 1996. One afternoon a friend asked Rose to pick up her car at Lou Guido's, a popular gym in Dana Point. Gyms aren't just a place to work out. They have their own subculture, complete with an area to cruise the available lot while expanding ones pecs or losing a few of those extra pounds added at the dinner table during the holidays. Also, a place to meet and for people who were alone while shedding pounds and feeling better, it was a perfect venue to let the eyes wander. Admiring the results of others, it motivates many to excel and subsequently sign up with a trainer to tone up or participate in a stretching class or aerobics. A social environment unlike others, its both hardcore and laid-back atmosphere is the perfect elixir to start a conversation or inquire about the certain someone on the tread mill. It was against this backdrop that she first saw a tall, handsome man with a broad-brimmed hat emerging from the gym. Rose describes herself as: "I'm a walker, not a gym person. I like to feel the wind and let loose walking along the beach or a pathway. That was one of the reasons I needed to be in California, not in some environment that kept you indoors. But the gym isn't my thing. It never was." But others used the facilities and needed both the motivational aspects of seeing others challenging themselves with yoga, weights or on treadmills. And yet others sought different ventures. Thus, like many spas and gyms, it also served as a meeting area to relax after a workout and sip a healthy concoction of overpriced protein shakes with names like the Velvet Elvis, Magilla Gorilla and Oreo Surprise.

Rose didn't know that the tall, black handsome man was the former heavyweight champ. It was a month later that she was introduced to him at a jazz venue called Salt Creek Grille. A typical Orange County restaurant overlooking the ocean, it served the usual prix fixe early bird specials with a continental cuisine. Thus, the salmon, trout and assorted meats such as ribs, steak and pork attracted the diners while listening to a live jazz quartet. One night, she again spotted the same tall, handsome man with a black fedora, dressed all in black. Black shoes, black pants, black shirt, black hat. "The only thing not black were his eyes and his teeth. I was unsure of him and didn't want to invade his space and eventually left. But he sure looked good!"

Yet, a few weeks later, Rose saw the tall figure again at Brio's, another watering hole and popular venue. She was finally introduced to him by Derek Bordeaux. Still not knowing who the famous boxer was, he shook her hand, announcing "I just fired my wife!" Rose recalls that she looked at him and smiled at this most unusual introduction and went on her way, adding: "Take care of yourself." A short time later, she again saw Ken at the Salt Creeke Grille. The attractive Rose was surrounded by a group of admirers but noticed the tall gentleman. Yes, the same one that she had seen before. "I later found out from Derek that Ken had spoken to him about me. Derek came up to me, acting no doubt as a matchmaker and said: 'He's been asking questions about you—such as 'is she single, married, does she have children?' The wheels started turning in my head and I asked myself: 'He's already into my business.' Before I uttered a sound, Derek then added: 'Do you know who he is?' He went on to laud his friend by telling me that the tall, handsome stranger was none other than the former heavyweight champion of the world, Mr. Ken Norton. I can still see the look on Derek's face when I said: 'I'm just a Louisiana country girl. So what if he's famous? Frankly, I couldn't care less about someone who was just trying to hit on me.' I can remember poor Derek listening to me say over the music that was blaring, 'I don't like boxing, don't like violence. My father and brothers would watch the fights on the TV, while us girls sat in the kitchen and dished the dirt on all topics that came and went.'"

What Rose failed to realize was the fact that Derek Bordeaux and Ken Norton were good buddies, a friendship that had cemented itself with Norton's love of Derek's music at the club. In fact, Ken Norton was a fixture at the club every Friday that he was fortunate enough to be in town and hear the jazz and 'mellow out' to the strains of the live music that at once put him at ease.

Within a few minutes, Rose saw Ken Norton walking towards her. "I now knew who the big guy was. Derek had spilled the beans and set up a meeting. Ken noticed me and before I knew it—we made eye contact and the rest is history."

Rose Conant distinctly remembers the crowd at another popular club—Justine's. "Before Ken and I made contact, fellows asked me to dance—especially the slow numbers. The slow numbers gave them a chance to hold tight, be tight and touch. Not for me! Yes, there was plenty of dancing, both to fast and slow music. And I love to dance, but I was on my guard with some of the guys just out for a good time, a one-nighter and I was always approached to dance and always refused the slow numbers. You might say I just wasn't comfortable and I guess a few of the regulars felt I was a snob. So be it!

"By the time Ken had approached me, the night was like most Fridays with a packed house and plenty of men asking single women to dance. I was asked and I refused to dance the slow ones. When Ken came up to me, I started to look around and said to myself, 'This man is not coming or is he?' My nerves were frayed enough and now this! Coming straight through the crowd like Moses parting the waters, I was getting more tense by the second. He finally made it through and came straight up to me. By now, my once nervous self managed to eke a smile and he said: 'I'm Ken. Let's dance.'" A slow dance tune was in progress, one that Rose had time and again avoided. Yet, she couldn't say no. Wouldn't say no. She recalls: "The slow number was still playing and the guys around Ken, the same ones who always wanted to dance, kept repeating to him: 'She won't dance a slow one with you.'" But this was Ken Norton, who had defeated the most formidable of them all and was not going to quit in this quest. To the onlookers, those rejected suitors, he had just one response: "That's the breaks—she'll dance with me!" In fact, Ken had asked Justin, the bandleader, to replay the same song—yes the same, slow song that required a close-up dance. But Rose didn't mind that it was a 'slow dance'. In fact, it was a way to ease the tension. Besides, it was time. Time to move on and meet someone. "And he was something!" She was smitten and danced with Ken. The tall stranger with the dimples and a smile that lit up the room was exactly what Rose needed. "When it was over, the entire floor erupted in applause and that was the momentous start of our relationship. We then sat and talked about nothing most of the night, until it came time to leave."

What Rose didn't know was that Ken was lonely and looking for a friend or a person of interest. He was an intriguing figure to Rose and she was an attractive, perky and vivacious woman who found her new friend not only attractive but also a challenge.

Rose asked herself: "How do I get this guy to loosen up and just chill out.

"After we danced and talked a bit, he got my phone number, indicating that he would call soon." Rose recalls she wasn't about to hold her breath, waiting for a call.

A few days later, true to his word, the phone rang at Rose's apartment, asking her to go to breakfast at Molly's, a diner a few miles away.

"Molly's, a diner and favorite spot for locals, is close to where I was living and it would be a neutral space and unassuming.

"I arrived at Molly's and within a few minutes Ken entered. He had his hat atop his head and he immediately came over to the table," Rose remembers.

"I figured he'd have a man-size breakfast—the works—pancakes, eggs, juice, sausage or bacon and toast." Norton, of course, had what he always ate since his childhood days in Jacksonville—Cheerios and bananas and whole wheat toast.

What started as a breakfast soon developed into a friendship then into a lasting relationship to this day. Rose Conant was the perfect candidate for the likes of Ken Norton— tough, suspicious, determined yet very loyal, trustworthy and above all, a most reliable person.

"I was incomplete without Rose. She arrived and thank God, she did. Before Rose, I was a waste." Tall, statuesque, with piercing eyes and great looks, she was a perfect match for Ken Norton. She stood out in a crowd and her mere presence caught the eye of many hungry suitors. Always attired in her best with her hair in perfect place, her gold chain completed the earrings and watch she wore. She was a steadfast, focused individual, a tribute no doubt to her hard upbringing in Louisiana and her sense of fair play as a product of her Catholic education. Her determination to meet him paid off and he asked her if she wanted a ride in his proud Mercedes.

"He loved his car and I said, 'Why not.' I think in some ways it was an extension of himself. A way to get onto the freeway and leave the confines of the house and let loose."

Rose noticed the gold bracelet that Ken always wore plus the boxing ring and another gold ring on his pinky plus a gold chain to complete the package.

"All that bling I thought could mean that the man liked fine things or just wanted to show off. At any rate, it was damn impressive and the real thing. I got into the car not knowing what to expect."

She recalls fastening her seat belt while he played some mellow mixes on the CD. "The interior was fresh smelling with a hanging fresh scent of vanilla dangling from the rear view mirror. He started the car and began to chat, just small talk."

Rose recalls: "I should have said no, as he nearly hit a mailbox! Maybe he was focusing too much into me, but he scared the hell of me."

For the next three years, Rose Conant and Ken Norton would meet, this time at Rose's home for lunch every day. Keeping to his new diet, he ate no red meat, just chicken or fish with green tea. "It's good for my bladder problem," he said to her once. The ritual of daily lunch was now something that the ex-boxer could look forward to and discuss issues and events that were going on in the world both near and far. The small talk that started in the car extended into a weekly ritual that both Rose and Ken looked forward to. But there was something that bothered her.

"I was intrigued by the fact that during this period, he never invited me to his house. I knew he was no longer with his wife, but I couldn't help but think that something told him not to get too friendly. I guess he felt he had been burned one too many times with the women in his life and I just resigned to the fact that we would meet on Saturdays and continue in whatever capacity he had in mind. He was good company but I had to think that there was much more to this man." Finally, Ken did get the nerve to invite her over and a new phase in their relationship began.

It wasn't until 2003 that Rose and Ken started to live together. Rose became his biggest supporter and chief confidant. She began to rearrange and set items of interest in the house in their respected places, beginning with the Trophy Room. What stood out at once was a 20 foot high picture of Norton plus Ali, Frazier and Holmes. In addition, the "Father of the Year," picture with his children occupied a special niche to the right of the four champions' picture. But, things were otherwise in disarray and needed to be arranged and categorized. Rose set out and accomplished a minor miracle. At once, she organized the myriad of newspaper and magazine articles and the assorted pictures of Ken in and out of the ring, including the many photos from his 20 films. "There must have been literally hundreds of articles, photos, and memorabilia of his glory days in boxing." Within a few months, the assorted items were catalogued, labeled alphabetically and arranged for anyone interested in the history of Ken Norton's boxing and acting career. Yet, Rose was much more than just a programmer and organizer. She provided Ken with a new lease on life and a reason to keep struggling despite his constant pain. Ever vigilant, she was the anchor who made sure that the proper medications were taken, appointments to doctors and associates were met and became, in a short period, his charges d'affaires in all matters of importance. A visit today to his home is highlighted by paying homage to the now famous Ken Norton Trophy Room. Complete with the belts he earned, are statuettes of the boxer, photos highlighting the 1973 win over Ali, and a full-length picture sans shirt as Mede in the steamy movie, *Mandingo*. In addition, there are plaques, citations and a host of letters from fans and dignitaries throughout the world. Rose knew the accolades were important and made sure that he was properly acclaimed. Like a shrine to a patron saint, it serves as a reminder of the great achievements of a great boxer.

"Rose has her way and knows what she's doing," Ken adds. She makes sure his shirts and ties match and gives a great deal of attention to grooming, as evidenced by her attention to neatness whenever Ken is out in the public eye. "He always looked great and color coordinated before I came onto the scene. Now it's just a continuation of that clean." She herself is immaculately attired, with matching ensembles of assorted suits, dresses, blouses and hair always in place. As a couple, they are recognized and appreciated in their orbit as well as on the road.

The focus of Ken's existence is his home and the people who inhabit it. Rose, his children and an occasional visit from Jacksonville by his mother, Ruth or his manager, Dr. Don Hennessey, Jr. are part of his world.

Ken learned to appreciate Rose and their relationship has

grown. Home is a very neat and comfortable surrounding with the famous Trophy Room a source of pride. Their home is their castle and, like many families, occupies the center of their universe. Life has been a series of events for them from attending boxing venues to fund-raisers in the area. Rose's contribution is amplified by the fact that she gets Ken out more often and is his biggest supporter and cheerleader. She has given him an added incentive to persevere. A real lady, a real lifeline and dedicated to Ken. As he often has said, "Rose changed everything. Before her, I wasn't whole. There was something missing." That link is now solid and Ken and Rose are a well known item in Orange County.

Chapter 11

Like every state, Illinois has a colorful license plate that advertises itself as its citizens traverse throughout America. A white-colored plate, with the motto: "Land of Lincoln," pays homage to the Great Emancipator who is interred in the cemetery in Springfield, the state's capital. Like most final resting places it is a source of curiosity and information, tracing the sad events from the assassination at Ford's Theater on April 14, 1865 to the railroad trip from Washington to Baltimore, Philadelphia, New York City, Albany and across upstate New York to Buffalo, Cleveland, Chicago and finally to Springfield. Along the way, the cortege stopped at the cities, allowing thousands to pay homage to their fallen hero. In New York City's famed Beaux Arts city hall, Lincoln lay in state. The procession that followed to the Hudson Train Station, as it was then known, at 30th Street and 9th Avenue, was witnessed, the New York Times estimated, by 120,000. Walt Whitman, famous Brooklyn resident was one of those who witnessed the sad array of horses, Union soldiers and the cortege, draped in black. Stores, shop windows, and banks had black bunting, as a final tribute from the nation's largest city. Walt Whitman, seeing the grieving masses did what he did best—he wrote a moving and lasting tribute on paper. In a eulogy, he was best able to capture the grief the nation was experiencing in his now famous poem: "O Captain, My Captain." Comparing the death of the president to the loss of a ship's captain made its readers feel that they too were part of a family journey united in grief at the loss of its leader. Not alone, but part of the greater throng. The Whitman poem at once became a source of honoring the fallen leader and helped ease the battle scarred nation to look beyond the pale of grief and finish the work that Lincoln had planned. Its poignant metaphoric lines ends:

"From fearful trip, the victor ship, comes in with object won;

Exult, O shores, and ring, O bells!

But I, with mournful tread,

Walk the deck my Captain lies,

Fallen cold and dead."

The citizens of Springfield have a unique and special bond to Lincoln. The Whitman poem, still memorized by many students in all 50 states, still exults a sense of pride in a person who displayed courage under fire in the greatest of conflicts. The people of Springfield have indeed much to be proud of and today, that same spirit of service to others is extended to those in greatest pain and need. Like thousands of cities and towns throughout the US, Springfield has its own heroes of the day in its hospitals and end-of-life care facilities, such as the St. John's Hospice.

Located on Carpenter Street in the state capital, St. John's is part of an institution started just a decade after its most famous citizen was interred, 1875. Their mission is one of compassion, respect, counseling, bereavement support and 24 hour care with staff that includes doctors, nurses, occupational and speech therapists and a host of volunteers from the greater community. Located just an hour east of Ken Norton's hometown of Jacksonville, St. John's Hospice gives a special quality of life care to those in the greatest need—the terminally ill patient and the family in need of support. Like any crisis facility, it tries to ease the burden of the inevitable and allows the dignity of both patient and family to be the prime focus of their mission.

In 2004, one of Ken Norton's boyhood friends, Don Hennessey, was diagnosed with stage four cancer that had spread to the liver. "There wasn't much hope and the doctors suggested, after an extensive stay in the cancer unit at St. John's that the family move Don to St. John's Hospice," his son and Ken Norton's manager, Don. Jr. recalled.

"Dad was very lucid and spoke a lot about his early years on Hackett Street with Ken. They were the same age and went to school together and were the best of friends."

Don Jr. wanted to make sure his dad was comfortable, knowing that the days were dwindling and that he and his mom, Marguerite and his dad's children (Willie, Eva, Linda and Crystal) and grandchildren could be there for him.

Don Jr. continues: "I had previously lined up a couple of appearances in Jacksonville, as I knew Ken would be there. I called and asked him to go to St. John's with me to visit dad.

I explained to Ken the condition he was in and told him not to expect too much from the visit, but that it would mean a lot to dad."

Ken Norton never hesitated and arrived with Don Jr. at the facility to a smiling Don Sr.

Ken recalls: "When I entered the room, I didn't know what to expect. I was told that my friend had a month or less and I wanted to be positive."

Exiting the elevator, Ken was ushered down the long hallway to Don Hennessey's room. The room reminded him of his long confinement in the hospital 18 years earlier. He knew what pain was all about and wanted to be there for a friend in need. Nodding to several aides who recognized the former boxer, he approached the room with his hand firmly gripping his cane, hat atop his head.

Entering the room, Ken remembers: "The room had several colorful balloons with the ususal get well wishes hanging from the ceiling as well as some cards taped on the wall to the left of his bed. To my amazement, Don was sitting up to the right of the bed, smiling broadly when he saw me walk into the room."

Don Hennessey's family had made every attempt to make his final days as comfortable as possible. The hospice facility in Springfield was well run and highly respected. The family, knowing that his final days would be painful and traumatic, felt the hospice would be the best avenue to take. He would have 24 hour care plus a staff that was dedicated and professional. Therefore, when the oncologist suggested that the hospice would be best for both family and Don Hennessey, the family agreed. So, the visit from his distant friend was a welcome sight to his bedside.

The small room with the white walls was typical of any hospital or hospice with a brown leather chair on each side of the bed. When Ken entered, the bed was propped up, making it easier to get in and out of bed with the least amount of difficulty. Don Hennessey, however, was not in his bed.

"The visit was a surprise and it just happened that Dad was sitting up, not in bed."

Don Jr. recalls: "When Ken entered, Dad was sitting up. Ken was surprised that he could still sit up and talk and be conversant and it made his day. The smile on his face said volumes. I left the room for a bit to allow them to trash over the old days in Jacksonville and to get myself together. Ken Norton got my dad to forget his pain and I was so grateful for that. For those few moments he was himself again, talking to his old buddy and getting a pat or two on the shoulder from the wounded warrior himself. Ken knew what pain was and how difficult it was to endure it. His presence at Dad's bedside on that sunny, breezy day was the best dose of medicine for Dad. He gave him some measure of comfort as his days were winding down to an inevitable end. I came back into the room and the two were smiling. We took a photo which shows a smiling Dad with his good friend Ken at his side. Ken knew what it was to endure pain from the car crash and my family never forgot the warm, human gesture. To this day, that photo is a prized possession of the Hennessey family."

Don Hennessey passed away two weeks later. His son remembers: "When we called Ken at his California home telling him the news, there was what seemed a long silence before he spoke." There was no need for Ken to say anything. That special visit to an old buddy on that warm, breezy afternoon did wonders. For Don Jr., it meant everything. For like his ailing father and the famous visitor, he had seen and endured an enormous tragedy just seven years earlier.

"When I see Ken Norton, I see a survivor like myself. He has quite a story to tell and so do I."

The younger Don Hennessey was with his sister Linda and his partner Rick on December 1, 1997 in suburban Green Bay, Wisconsin at the nearby Oneida Casino in the town of Ashwaubindan. The famous town of the Superbowl champions, Green Bay Packers was just a few miles away. But the lure of the casino was the reason for the trek, not the now intense playoffs in the NFL. Like any casino players, they played the slot machines, had dinner and not finding the event very profitable, decided to leave within a few hours. "It was getting late and I wanted to leave," Don recalls. The addictive slots and blackjack tables had done their job and deprived the group of any fortune to be made that night. The warm and multicolored lights of the slots gave way to a cold Wisconsin night. So, the three occupants of the car, on Packard Land Drive, drove off and stopped at a red light just one block away. It was 1:45AM.. It happened in an instant!

"We were rear-ended at the light by a speeding 60 mph car. My sister at the time was 270 lbs. She was sitting next to me in the front. My partner Rick Collins was in the back."

Don goes on to explain the horrific minutes in detail following the crash: "Every minute of the crash is vivid in my mind. I looked in the rear-view mirror and there was nothing. I looked back a couple of seconds later but it was too late to do anything but look in horror at the speeding vehicle coming up behind in the rear-view mirror to the impact. That dreadful crunch, the noise, the flying debris and the stench of gasoline. My sister sitting to the right was unconscious. At first, I thought she was dead. Her eyes were closed and she wouldn't answer. I knew something had to be done and done right now. The car burst into flames upon impact. I could feel the heat and the smoke was blinding me. That horrible stench of gas I remember too. I don't know what drove me, but I was able to pull my heavy sister across the driver's seat and out of the vehicle. She would only have minor injuries, thank God. The flames were now shooting into the air some 50 feet and caught the attention of Skycam, the local Green Bay news affiliate. I also remember trying to save Rick as the flames kept getting closer and hotter. Hotter and closer. I tried to pull him out and succeeded half way. I couldn't do any more. The adrenalin was there, but I couldn't remove him. My attempts to get him out made me more determined, yet the car was now totally engulfed in flames. I remember being pulled by some first responders. I wanted to get Rick out. He didn't say anything, but his eyes were opened. With the arrival of the paramedics, the car's flames were shooting into the air. I was tackled onto a stretcher and sped off to St. Vincent's Hospital in Green Bay."

First responders were amazed that Don Hennessey was able to accomplish what he did for he had sustained life-threatening injuries to himself. What happens in these situations are written up in medical journals. They defy logic. Like the miracles at Fatima or Lourdes, they have no rational explanation. It's the human drive to save another, like a soldier in combat. Similar situations have been recorded and discussed both professionally and for the greater good. For instance, the mother who lifts a car when seeing her young son hit under a wheel; the will to survive of a person on life-support who refuses to succumb or the unexplained awakening of a patient from a comatose state after years. This was one of those seminal moments for Don. It would change him and his life forever. His injuries were, like Ken Norton's eleven years earlier, life-threatening. Not only did surgeons open up his chest, placing vital chest tubes to breathe but also he had broken every rib in his rib cage! Not a good prognosis for anyone, young or old. In addition, due to his heroic efforts to extricate Rick, he had both lungs collapsed and suffered second and third degree burns on his right side as the flames started to engulf the car. Placed in intensive care, he would have to be monitored for infections and quarantined for a time. Yet Don, like his hero Ken Norton, was tough and wouldn't give up. He responded well to the treatments and was soon able to breathe on his own albeit with some difficulty.

Don Hennessey, Jr. remained in intensive care for some 15 to 20 days. Slowly, he was able to breathe on his own and was allowed family visitors once every two hours wearing masks to protect him from infections so often prevalent with recovering burn victims. Ever so slowly he was able to connect to his surroundings—the bed, the myriad of cards that had been sent, the balloons that his family sent. He began to go over and over in his mind what he could have done differently to save Rick. Deep inside, he knew he had done all he could, yet it hurt. The emotional disappointment was overwhelming and needed to be addressed. He knew it. The doctors and staff did as well.

"I knew I was an emotional train wreck as well, having let Rick down." Or had he?

"Doctors and nurses were amazed at the fact, that despite the injuries, I was able to rescue my sister and try to save Rick. Rick died. I felt I had let him down. What could I have done differently?"

We read of people who survive catastrophic events, such as a plane crash, car accident or an act of God, such as a hurricane or tornado. Stories of someone who dies sitting next to you in a plane crash or a car accident or is thrown by nature's force into the atmosphere during a tornado and is later found dead, are told over and over. Yet the survivors wonder: "Why did I make it? Why didn't he?" This survivor's guilt had to be dealt with and the staff at St. Vincent's spoke to Don to reassure him that there was nothing more he could have done. Rick had suffered a broken pelvis and had already succumbed to his injuries despite the herculean efforts he had made. He did not die from the inferno engulfing the car. Indeed, even the medical reports were given to him not only to vindicate this fact but also to reassure him that what he had done was heroic and gallant. Yet, the events of that early morning would stay with him forever.

"I felt somewhat relieved to know that Rick died not from the burning wreckage, but from the impact and I was able to start resting a bit better once released from the hospital and recuperating at my parents' home in Cedar Rapids. I stayed on the couch, read a lot and eventually, with assistance, started walking. My mom would come in every morning and make sure I was comfortable, took my medications, help me dress and would be there for me. Suddenly the smell of coffee or eggs frying was a welcome sight and I started to get myself on the road to recovery. I thought of writing a journal and expressing my thoughts, fears and objectives for recovery, but instead read a bit, watched TV, visited with friends and started to get back into life. Yet, the thought of that late night and early morning left me still empty for the longest time."

Despite the pain, he was determined to get well. And get well, he did!

What followed were years of therapy—painful physical therapy as well as counselors who alleviated the internal grief inside him. Much like Ken Norton, he had to decide what avenue to follow and like his father's friend, he decided he was a survivor and set out to rally and get well. It would take months of counseling, soul searching, visits to Rick's grave and eventually coming to terms with harsh reality. He got stronger and today has fully recovered but never forget that December night in Wisconsin.

Yet he was not the type to brood and want sympathy from others. His strength got him through the worst crisis of his life and made him stronger. His heroism also did not go unnoticed.

For his brave efforts, Don Hennessey Jr., was awarded by

Governor Tommy Thompson of Wisconsin the Certificate of Heroism. Actions by individuals tell us so much of a person's character. Don inherited a sense of fair play, good morale and the willingness to stand and fight for your beliefs from his parents. He wouldn't let the memory of Rick die and he wanted all the details of the person who rear-ended him. What he found out made him an advocate for justice.

The individual who rammed his car at the excessive speed and caused such destruction of life and property was a female driver charged with DWI. Eventually charged with 12 counts, including vehicular homicide, driving under the influence of alcohol and depraved indifference to human life. Don made it a point, despite both the physical and emotional scars, to attend court proceedings, making the long trip from Cedar Rapids to Green Bay. Eventually, like most court cases, plea bargaining was offered and she was sentenced to 10 years. The painful fact is that the person who caused such havoc served a mere 4 years in prison.

Four years for the life of Rick. It made no sense to Don. That painful night transformed him to avoid alcohol and be supportive of DWI and DUI legislation his state. He has come to terms and has found closure and moved on and yet, still has the night of December 1, 1997 with him every day.

After his father died in 2004, Don became more interested in Ken Norton's legacy and took over responsibilities to head Ken Norton Enterprises in 2007. He found in the boxer a surrogate father who has been both supportive and there for him. They speak nearly every day and exchange emails and calls. Don's expertise is apparent from a solid record of business management over the years.

"When I took over the management of the enterprise, I made sure that all communications would come to me first.

Sound management was needed and I stepped up to the plate. Important vouchers, data and other pertinent material needed fixing. Aside from the financial aspects, it's the networking with companies, former boxers and sponsors that motivates me." It motivated Don to sponsor events with Ken Norton's name attached to them. Sending a fan a letter or autographed picture of the former fighter, Don can be relied on. His dedication to Ken Norton and his legacy is paramount and he has given both survivors a common bond.

Whenever a youngster wants an autographed picture of Ken or a boxing fan wants to get information, Don is there. Like a steady rock in place, he micro manages the business affairs of the company and lets no one step in the way. The bespeckled, balding middle age man is a dynamo who won't let others interfere or disrupt what he has built. Thus, the company known as Ken Norton Enterprises is intent on keeping memorabilia, documents relating to newspaper and magazine articles, books and photos to be catalogued and recorded. He and Ken Norton have established a friendship akin to the one that his father and Ken enjoyed.

Don Hennessey and Ken Norton were both at death's door. But fate would not have its way. There's a greater mission and story to be told of both of these warriors and they are proof positive of an inner strength in all of us. Their willingness to carry on has enriched the lives of those they hold dear.

Chapter 12

Before the railroads there were the canals. The Transportation Revolution in the young republic had its origins in 1817 with the construction of the famed Erie Canal, a canal that brought New York City to its premiere status as the biggest commercial center of the young nation. A brainchild of De Witt Clinton, the Erie Canal began at the confluence of the Hudson and Mohawk Rivers in upstate New York in Waterford, across the Hudson from Troy. Extending from Waterford, it meandered across the Mohawk Valley and ended some 363 miles later in Tonawanda in western New York, near Buffalo. A marvel of its day 40 feet wide, four feet deep with 85 locks, it served as a catalyst for the completion of other notable canals, such as the Cumberland and the Champlain. The Champlain Canal wound its way further north in upstate New York through small towns like Mechanicville, Ft. Edward, and Hudson Falls, eventually connecting to towns adjoining Lake George and onto Lake Champlain and the Canadian border. Along the famed Erie Canal, cities sprouted up along its route, such as Rochester and the economy quickly prospered, providing jobs for the hearty and a sense of adventure for the young. Imagine what it was like to see the barges full of passengers venturing into the unknown reaches beyond western New York State to find a new life. They, along with the non-English speaking immigrants, occasional vagabonds, assorted drifters, schemers and dreamers, found a friend to fulfill their dreams. The canal was not just a mode of transport; it symbolized the freedom to achieve that sense of adventure, replete with its wonders and dangers. It was part of the American folklore. The canal would stand the test of time. With the completion of the canal in 1825, De Witt Clinton, now governor of New York, presided proudly over the 'Marriage of the Waters,' pouring a pail of Lake Erie water from Buffalo into New York City harbor. Moments later, boats now using steam and able to go upstream since the successful run of the Robert Fulton's Clermont in 1807, began their trek up the Hudson and onto the great canal. Thus began the first great migration out west as well as the first network of rural and urban America that brought grains, meat and textiles to all corners of the state. Once in Buffalo, the Great Lakes were used by those hardy pioneers who ventured even further west into Ohio, Indiana, Illinois, Michigan and Wisconsin. Stories were written and songs were sung about the Erie Canal. News was transmitted before Mr. Morse's telegraph in 1844 by many of the burly bargers who worked the canal. And work hard they did! Along with the song and dance and news, some of the workers needed a diversion so bare-knuckle boxing events came about. People would flock to the center town green or makeshift area for these events. These sporting events gave the locals a chance to gather and chat and witness an event that, no doubt, would be the subject at the dinner table. Rough, raw and like the pioneers moving west, these boxing matches gave the crowds along the route in towns like Utica, Rome and Lockport the chance to witness a sport that was becoming more and more popular. Long before the Marquis de Queensbury of Britain rules gave boxing a set of guidelines, it was every man for himself. Whoever stood the test of time and was not bloodied and thrown to the ground emerged the victor. Rounds were endless and one can imagine the damage the body blows achieved when they hit their mark. So, the canal became not just a mode of transport but rather the network to meet, exchange ideas, trade and yes, witness an occasional boxing event. It helped the young nation come together in the aftermath of the War of 1812 and was both an engineering and commercial success. Transporting, communicating and networking all rolled into one, gave the canal a unique role in the nation's glorious past. The faster railroad soon eclipsed the canal ride, but it remained uniquely a part of the fabric of America. Looking like a Currier and Ives painting, the children running along-side the barge, the women and men waiting for an arrival of a special sister or niece or nephew, the folks on the boat scanning to be recognized, gave this unique spectacle a script all its own. Thanks to the network of canals throughout the eastern and central part of the US, migration and settlement owe much to the canal adventure.

One of the smaller yet notable towns along the canal where these bare-knuckle fights took place was Canastota, in Central New York, a short distance from Syracuse. Settled in 1810, today it is a tourist destination on a par with the Baseball Hall of Fame in nearby Cooperstown, New York, the Football Hall of Fame in Canton, Ohio and the Basketball Hall of Fame in Springfield, Massachusetts. What lures the tourist is an annual induction ceremony at the International Boxing Hall of Fame founded in 1982 by two notable citizens of Canastota: Carmen Basilio and his nephew Billy Backus. These two world champion boxers wanted a fitting tribute to the boxing world's greats of past, present and future. Basilio, both a welter and middleweight champion of the 1950's and Backus, a welterweight champion in both 1970 and 1971, made the small town, known for its Victorian houses, Canal Town Museum, Carnegie library on the National Registry of Historic Places and factories that produced specially-made cut glass, the repository of boxing world archives. So it was that when the 25th anniversary of Basilio's victory of Sugar Ray Robinson for the middle-weight title neared, a group of Canastota's citizens, felt a tribute should be in the offing.

Within a few years, money was raised and grants given by the State of New York, resulting in what is today the International Boxing Hall of Fame. According to Ed Brophy, the executive director, "many of Canastota's residents put their energies behind the effort to establish the International Boxing Hall of Fame." Two state grants totaling $50,000 plus pledges from local residents of $1,000 each, made the dream a reality. Four years later, a 2,000 square-foot facility was opened for the public to enjoy and learn. The efforts of hard-working people in the community plus a vision to retain memorabilia from pictures, boxing gloves, ticket stubs, recordings of bouts and biographies of the inductees, all make the Boxing Hall of Fame an attraction as noteworthy as any of the other sports' venues.

According to Brophy, "Many of the visitors like the photos but also the robes worn by the likes of Ali, Frazier and Norton. Joe Louis' prized purple trunks or Rocky Marciano's gloves worn when he fought Jersey Joe Walcott are favorites."

In the official record book entitled, "Boxing Register," by James B. Roberts and Alexander G. Skutt, the authors credit the town's residents, such as Joe Bonaventura and Farrell Miller as being instrumental in forming the Hall of Fame. An article in the *Canastota Bee-Journal*, lauding Basilio's silver anniversary served as a catalyst in making the hall of fame a reality. "That the Canastota area had also produced another champion in Backus, as well as strong welterweight contender Dickie DiVeronica—ranked eighth-best in the weight division in the early 1960's, gave the town something to crow about." Thus the movement was started to begin fund-raising and find sponsors.

The International Boxing Hall of Fame was dedicated in 1984. Since its opening major expansions have occurred, including a new library.

The Hall of Fame library also has for the student of boxing, boxing magazines, newspaper articles of famous bouts, statistics on the fighters' records and of course, a good gift shop to take something home. Its website aptly states its mission as follows: "Honor and preserve boxing's rich heritage and provide an educational experience for our many visitors."

What a visitor finds is a complete history of international boxing divided into five categories: Modern, Old-Timers, Pioneer, Non-Participant and Observer. Roberts and Skutt explain further in "Boxing Register:" "The voters hail from all parts of the globe, including Australia, South Africa, Italy and all other parts of Europe, Canada, Argentina, Japan and of course, the US." In order to be considered for entry into the prestigious roster, candidates have to pass a pre-screening committee consisting of boxing historians. The Register goes on to explain: "Modern fighters are additionally required to have been retired for five years. In order to be enshrined into the Hall of Fame, candidates are chosen by 150 boxing experts, historians and writers."

Walking into this special place is a walk through history itself, replete with the ups and downs of a sport that only a true boxing fan can appreciate. The Pioneers of Boxing include the great John L. Sullivan and Paddy Duffy, tough Irishmen who fought their way out of poverty and into the limelight of bare-knuckles boxing, like the bouts entertaining the towns along the Erie Canal. In addition, the 1908 fight between the first black heavyweight, Jack Johnson and Tommy Barnes, the 'Great White Hope' in Sydney,

Australia, is highlighted. This fight later became the basis for the academy award winning movie with James Earl Jones. With his white, teenage wife, Johnson fled first to Canada and then to Europe to escape the obvious racial hostility and to avoid an arrest on the grounds of transporting a minor for immoral reasons across state lines. A visitor to the Hall of Fame can see historic fights, such as the Joe Louis and Max Schelling fight at the old Madison Square Garden on 50th Street where Louis' win made him an international star, defeating the fellow heavyweight from Nazi Germany. Roberts and Skutt describe a first-timers visit as follows: "Once you walk through the doors of the International Boxing Hall of Fame, you are immediately thrown into a colorful and unforgiving world of flesh and flash." One of the major exhibits is the 'Wall of Fame' where each inductee is represented with a plaque, including a photo and a brief biography. Of course, the most popular attractions are the artifacts of the boxing venues: championship belts donated by the inductees, plaster casts of famous fists, robes, boxing gloves and the great photos of bouts.

In 1992, Ken Norton was inducted into the International Boxing Hall of Fame. It was only a matter of time before they would honor one of the greats of the sport. Along with Norton, such honors were given to 28 others, such as: Nino Benvenuti, the 1960 Italian Gold medalist and middle weight; Eder Jofre, the great Brazilian bantam weight champ; Billy Graham, called the "uncrowned welterweight champion"; Charley Burley; Alexis Arguello; Ali's trainer, Angelo Dundee and boxers of the past such as: James Figg, Jem Belcher, James Burke, Tom King and Tom Spring. Many of the pioneer boxers, long gone, were nevertheless, enshrined that June date along with Norton to make the history a complete one.

Ken Norton arrived at the upstate hall of fame after a long flight from Los Angeles. The crowded events of the weekend started on June 4th with a barbeque sponsored by American Legion Post #140. "This was a great start to a memorable weekend. It reminded me of the summers in my small town. We thought it was going to rain, but the sky was soon clear. The food and smell of the beef, pork, Italian sausage and the homemade pies were all I needed to remind me of the old days when I was a kid in Jacksonville", Ken recalled. Although he no longer ate red meat, the aroma, especially from the Italian sweet sausage with onions and garlic, gave the venue a gastronomical fete, enticing everyone to the tables set up neatly under the maple trees. Norton was able, he recalls, to enjoy the desserts, salads and chicken and made good on his promise to avoid, despite their seductive aroma, the lure of the barbequed ribs and pork, while reacquainting with old boxing buddies and promising to sign picture autographs and boxing gloves in the events to follow.

The next day, Friday, started off with a Father/Son cookout followed by a press conference at the Museum Bandstand. "The conference lasted just 30 minutes and was a photo-op for the local and sports press covering the weekend events. We got off a few one liners and had a good time."

The rest of the day was a private tour of the facility, complete with a special stop at the imposing Hall of Fame with its plaques of the great pugilists of the world, now immortalized in bronze.

Ken recalls that evening, following a dinner at the Moose Lodge with a display of boxing billed as "Amateur Celebrity Boxing Night" at Canastota High School. Boxing promoter Ray Rinaldi brought the likes of Vinny Pazienza (Vinny Paz), then the junior middleweight champion along with the great Hector 'Macho' Comacho. In addition, local boxing clubs from nearby Herkimer, Syracuse, Rochester and Buffalo were on hand, thanks to the efforts of Rinaldi. The *Canastota Bee-Journal* recorded the event: "At 6PM, Camacho did his warm-ups in the ring before going a few rounds with of his sparing partners. Always a tease, he gave the audience a good show with his agility in the ring, the quick movement in his feet and the ever-surprising jabs. It was theater and the audience was his and his alone. After Camacho, Pazienza, recovering from a broken neck in an accident, worked out in the ring and worked on the bags and skipped rope. His presence was a coming-out of sorts from his injury and he was also well received by the adoring fans. The amateur boxers from the area were next and then Carmen Basilio got into the ring with his old foe, Gene Fullmer. Despite the 'drubbing' by these old war horses, the brief sparing and the wave to the crowd, the referee declared a draw to the roar of the sympathetic audience. Former heavyweight champ, Ken Norton even assisted a local photographer by grabbing her camera and taking his own pictures when she wasn't paying attention." This playful side of Norton was also there throughout the weekend when he told the waitress at Graziano's, across the street from the Hall of Fame to give an admiring customer his check!

Norton was having a good time. This was his hour to shine along with the other inductees. He certainly deserved it. On Saturday, following a golf tournament, a Hall of Fame Festival was held which included rides for the youngsters plus games and of course, refreshments. A more stately ceremony was held later that evening at the Museum with a cocktail reception followed by a Celebrity Photo Session and the Banquet of Champions Dinner at the Rusty Rail.

Sunday, June 7th was the date that the inductees would get their recognition. The day began with a breakfast at the

Hall of Fame followed by 'Casting of Champion Fists' at the local bandstand. The induction ceremony was followed by the Parade of Champions and finally a farewell cookout on the Festival Grounds. Celebrities from the entertainment and sports worlds have served as Grand Marshals for the parade, including such names as Mr. T, John Amos, Sherman Hemsley, Danny Aiello, Ryan O'Neal, Tony Orlando and Bo Derek. In 2005, big Hollywood stars such as the 'Gladiator', Russell Crowe and Daniel Day-Lewis, of Scorcese's 'Gangs of New York' were on hand.

Norton's record was impressive: NABF heavyweight title with Ali; another NABF title in 1975 with Jerry Quarry and he was awarded the WBC when he defeated Jimmy Young in 1977, the same year he KO'd Duane Bobick in the first round. Later that same year, he was awarded by the Boxing Writers' Association, the title of 'Fighter of the Year.' Here was a fighter who had fought Ali, Foreman, Shavers and Cooney and remained a gentleman and respected competitor. Norton was clad in a paisley shirt with a black baseball cap with an 'X' in tribute to Spike Lee's blockbuster on Malcolm X that would premiere later that year. Norton, ever an impressive figure at 6'3", was still in great shape despite his careful gait due to the 1986 accident and yet towered over all the other inductees. "I was the biggest and the best looking!" he boasted. He was right on both counts.

Each inductee spoke briefly and thanked the committee for their recognition in the prestigious club. In his autobiography, *Going the Distance*, Ken recalls what he said when it was his turn to speak. Ever the one with quick wit, he turned to fellow-inductee Angelo Dundee and said to the roar of the crowd: "My bank account grew out of my association with Ali. Thank you to my friend Angelo". While he was speaking he glanced at the other inductees on the platform with him and noticed that Alexis Arguello, the three-time champion pretended to be asleep. Norton wouldn't let the moment pass adding: "Aaron Pryor whipped his butt pretty good in Miami." That comment woke up Alexis right away. Norton was very pleased that two of his ex-boxing buddies were there for him: the ever courteous George Chuvalo and the bar-brawling Chuck Wepner. This was his weekend to shine and he performed brilliantly. Never one to complain, despite the constant pain from his accident, Norton remained a positive, upbeat and happy ex-warrior among his peers. His presence gave the events a special jolt of life and he was the star performing at his best. He has traveled back to the Hall of Fame for other ceremonies and has stayed in touch with the individuals who have given life to this great venue.

Chapter 13

It was 1:30 P.M. The new president, Ronald Reagan, was addressing the AFL-CIO at the Washington Hilton, the serpentine double-arched shaped hotel on Connecticut Avenue. Both rank and file and union officials were eager to hear the new president and his new albeit controversial economic plan of trickle-down economic policy. Waving and smiling broadly as the news media took photos, the former actor, used to his role, took his assigned place and began to speak. Greeted warmly, within minutes he combined fiscal policy with a few anecdotes so noteworthy of the Great Communicator. The hotel itself, built on top of the hill in the adjoining DuPont and Adams Hay neighborhood, stood prominently as a showcase when built in the 1960's. In the ensuing two decades since its completion, it was still a favorite, as it was today, complete with conference rooms in its lower floor and several ballrooms that were available for conferences, dances and assorted business for arriving conventioneers, such as the AFL-CIO. After they had dined on chicken, salad and dessert, it was time for Mr. Reagan to head back to the affairs of state. By 2:30 PM, the president finished his remarks and started toward the exit, shaking a few hands of the delegates, nodding to the staff, winking at a few who had given him a high five and then he was ushered to an awaiting motorcade to take him back to the White House. Then it happened!

No one saw him coming. No one. Not the hotel staff at

the Washington Hilton nor the ever-vigilant Secret Service had any way to detect the troubled young man lurking outside the hotel's side entrance on T Street that March morning in 1981. Hidden among the crowd, John Hinkley saw the new President, emerging from the side entrance of the hotel and, without much effort, got off six bullets, before being subdued by both the DC police and the Secret Service. Before it was over, four people had been hit: the president, his press secretary, Jim Brady and two DC officers. All of these terrible events occurred within six seconds and were recorded forever by the national press. Brady, the most severely wounded, took a bullet to the temple. The gun, a Rohm steel revolver, purchased at a Dallas pawn shop, had reached its intended target. The President was pushed into his limousine and when he started experiencing difficulty in breathing and spitting blood, was rushed to a nearby hospital with a bullet that had ricocheted off the side of the limo and entered under his left arm, grazing a rib and lodging just a few centimeters from his heart. Walking into the hospital, he collapsed and was immediately ushered into the operating room, the bullet having traveled close to his heart. His eventual recovery and return to his duties gave a bit of theater to the former actor in his most challenging role. His spunk, good humor and determination to resume his duties reassured the nation that he was in command. Regardless of ideology, the nation rallied and wished him well.

No mention of that near-fatal encounter can be found today at the Hilton. No plaques or pictures or commendations to the staff or DC police for gallantry can be found. Instead, the hotel is intent on performing its functions to visitors and arriving delegates for the myriad of conventions it hosts each year. Yet, the side exit on T Street is often gazed at and newcomers, ever aware of history, ask the question: "Is this where Reagan was shot?"

A different type of survivor is honored instead at the Hilton once a year in early November. Survivors not of a sudden bullet but of the boxing ring that have endured a sport that is at once both controversial and alluring. The boxers of the past meet, exchange stories and anecdotes of the past and renew old acquaintances from near and far. Aging pugilists that they are, they remain a special fraternity that has no equal. Their presence is at once sought and their advice, solicited or not, is there for all to absorb. The stories of the ring coupled with the victories and losses are recreated both on the wide screen or in tributes to those so lucky to be cited. They are introduced to the power that is only found in the nation's capital—CEO's of major Fortune 500 companies, municipal officials from the mayor to members of City Council and to the men and women that make up the federal government from representatives to senators and ambassadors. This once-a-year event is held not to assist errant or dysfunctional fighters and their families, but instead is totally devoted to the children of Washington and neighboring Maryland and Northern Virginia. Aptly named, 'Fight for Children', its mission is to bring together these former gladiators of the ring and in turn, raise thousands for the most needy—the children.

Fight Night, as indicated in the glossy program distributed to all benefactors, was started in 1990 by business and civic leader, Joseph E. Roberts, Jr., Chairman and CEO of J.E. Roberts Co. Its mission is: "to inform and guide policymakers, philanthropists and business leaders involved with education and healthcare initiatives." Quite an agenda! It advocates for policies and programs that deliver positive results. Attention to detail in dispensing funding to agencies in need, to be cited at its annual gala is an honor many seek. In addition, Fight for Children's organizers point out that they present "awards to local healthcare and educational non-profit organizations who demonstrate a positive impact on low-income children living in DC." So the "Fight for Children" is a nice linkage of business and education coming together for a common cause. What better avenue to use than to raise funds for programs such as Big Brothers, Big Sisters; Children's National Medical Center; the JFK Center for the Performing Arts/National Symphony Orchestra Education Program; Junior Achievement of DC; Latino Student Fund; Juvenile Diabetes Research Foundation; the DC Archdiocese Tuition Assistance Program; Alexandria Boxing Club; Mary's Center; Shepherd Foundation and the Latin American Youth Center. Quite a list of sponsors and recipients. Business, philanthropy and civic pride all in one neat package.

Guests arrived at the front entrance or at the now more infamous T Street entrance that witnessed the awful events of that March 1981 morning. Yet tonight, all eyes were on the former gladiators who made their profession, controversial and bloody as it may be, the focus of their energy. Taking a photo with one of the honorees was a special part of the night.

The chairman of the 2007 Fight Night was Charles Kuhn. Along with his co-chair, fellow businessman, Frederick D. Shaufeld, they proudly pointed out that since its inception "more than $76 million in corporate, individual and foundation support has occurred". So, the festivities that occurred in the ballroom of the Hilton on Connecticut Avenue become a black tie affair with a boxing ring thrown in the center for the admiring patrons! Thus it was that former greats of the ring who could make the trek to DC were introduced: Hector 'Macho' Camacho; 'Gentleman' Cooney; James 'Buster' Douglas; Roberto 'Mano de Piedra' Duran; 'Smokin' Joe Frazier, Jake 'Raging Bull' La Motta;

Ray 'Boom Boom' Mancini; Aaron 'The Hawk' Pryor; Earnie Shavers; Michael 'The Spinks Jinx' Spinks and of course, Ken 'The Champ' Norton. Each of these boxers, unique individuals with their own stories, were united on stage for a common cause. Like candidates at a convention, after a raucous and divisive primary season, they were ready to show solidarity. Boxing, like any sport, has its heroes and villains. Yet, no one introduced to the temporary ring that evening was out for self-glory. They were honored for their commitment to assist those in most need. Many of them, like LaMotta, Camacho, Shavers, Cooney and Norton knew what sacrifice was and the rough path to the top. Their legacy meant much, yet they wanted to make a difference and Fight Night was an avenue that provided them with respect and appreciation from the corporate and political worlds.

Each of the ex-boxers was introduced after a lazer show highlighting the various sponsors' contribution to the field of education. Ted Nugent, internationally known rock singer, led the entertainment with a uniquely heavy guitar-based National Anthem and as the ex-boxers were introduced, each of them was given the customary summary of their accomplishments to sustained approval from the black-tie crowd. Ken Norton's great 1973 rout of the Greatest was presented to sustained applause. Dressed to the 'nines', the tall, handsome fighter, now approaching 65, still retained his stature despite the challenges he faced since that fateful night in 1986.

Moguls of industry, fans of boxing, advocates and educators were united in a common cause for the most needy of the students in our nation's capital. The most emotional moment was the formal induction of 86 year-old Jake La Motta, the Raging Bull, into the Hall of Fame. It was pointed out that the scrappy New York street fighter had the guts

to go it all the way. Born in 1921 in the Bronx, he epitomized the tough, raw streets of that New York neighborhood
where he grew up. Scenes from the acclaimed Academy
Award-winning role of Robert De Niro in "Raging Bull'
were shown and Jake was escorted into the make-shift ring.
Still strong at 86, he walked unassisted to the center to the
cheers of the elite DC crowd that included the mayor and
other local officials. Cameras, cell phone photos and waves
of applause greeted him. Waving to the crowd, it was his
moment to shine and shine he did. Charles Kuhn, in award-
ing the honor to La Motta, indicated: "He made a steadfast
commitment to helping children in need. He is indeed one
of the greatest." It was an emotional moment for an aging
ex-boxer who graciously accepted the honor to the cheers of
his fellow ex-boxers on stage. La Motta was the perfect
choice - the old immigrant son who made it the hard way
just like all boxers, young and old; hours in the gym, the
constant routine of sparing, jumping rope, learning defensive strategies and out distancing your opponent by sheer
determination, grit and a sense of pride. La Motta had all of
these traits which made him a champion in every sense. His
award as a patron to the causes of education made this immigrant Italian's son realize that he had achieved that measure
of success which we call hero. With a record of 106 fights,
83 wins and just 19 losses and 4 draws, he was the indeed the
'Bronx Bull.' With so many fights under his belt, he was the
perfect candidate to cite.

"I fought other kids just for my dad's entertainment and
ended up a boxer. Those were the days when we would have
street brawls and people would bet who would come out a
winner." But it wasn't just the opponents in the ring with
which he had to come to terms. The Raging Bull, forced to
throw a fight, indeed, ordered to do so at his own peril ended
up testifying before a House committee on organized crime.

Fearing for his family's safety, he had no choice. Yet, through it all, he retained his sense of dignity and knew what it took to make a fighter. Long after his tenure was over in the ring, he went back to the same Bronx neighborhood, now largely black and Hispanic and set up the Jake La Motta Baseball Team in the shadow of Yankee Stadium. Like Norton, he wanted to give something back to the neighborhood he loved. And, like Ken Norton, later got a role with Paul Newman in "The Hustler" as the bartender. "No sexy role for me, but I gave it a shot and they liked it." No wonder this unique icon was recognized that night. Like Ken Norton, he was not just a boxer but an advocate. Like Norton, he had to endure difficult personal trials. And like Ken Norton, he ended up in a starring role not only in the ring but on the big screen. As was the case with Ken Norton, he was there to share his story that night to all the fancy gowns and coiffed hair and the CEO's who, watching the grand highlights on the screen, got only a measure of the sweat, discipline, sacrifice and pain it took to make a champion in the ring. All the other honorees knew what the road was like including the youngest, 45 year old Camacho, the 'playboy cutie' who was a terror in the ring. Undefeated for 11 years in six different weight classes. No other boxer can come near to that record. Tonight, like the aged fellow Bronx fighter La Motta, Camacho and his other buddies on stage, including Norton, were smiling and joking and perhaps a bit amused at all the fanfare. Quite a fraternity indeed!

On stage, all of the inductees were given an ovation. An ovation not only for their skills in the ring but also for lending their support to the neediest—the children. Through their own rough and tumble experience, they wore the reminders of a sport they had given their all to. The broken noses, limbs and battered ribs now tested by the years, gave these unique fraternity members an honor that was both fitting and appropriate. The program auctioned off some of the prized artifacts of their careers—from pictures of historic fights to robes and gloves. All for the children. All for charity. Their journey to the ring was as much an odyssey and adventure as any American story. Regardless of their age, race, or background, this unique group could stand tall, knowing how much they entertained America through the nation's own conflicts from depression to war to the fight for racial equality. They allowed us to pause in awe at their own 'dance of the ring' and showed us what hard work, persistence and fortitude really meant. Gritty, raw, tough in the ring, they had proven themselves time and again, often ignored and used by unscrupulous managers. They had much to be proud of and the adoring crowd knew they were in the presence of legends. Regardless of your opinion of the sport, Americans love their heros and this assemblage was as good as it gets. Better still, they like a good story that ends well and this is one that was destined to be remembered. These tough, once-hard bodies had their soft side and lent their energy, time and love to those children in need. Somewhere in the classrooms of Washington and the surrounding area, a youngster is watching the news. He or she sees the highlights and wonders: "Why not me?" A future Ken Norton or Jake LaMotta is out there and the drive and love of the sport of boxing, like any sport, is intoxicating. "How do I get started? What do I need to do? Where do I go? What will mom say about it?" That same youngster will remember what was showcased at the Hilton on that November night and a dream will be born. He'll bury his head in books, magazines, watch reruns of fights at the old Garden and see a host of immortals from Louis, Ali, Norton, Tyson and Marciano. He won't stop until he gathers all the information. Chores, friends and movies will take a back seat to this insatiable hunger. Projects in school will center on a bout between Norton and Ali and he'll hit the Internet to learn as much as he can of his newly found hero. Who will I be like? That hunger! His drive will keep him focused on his dream and what a dream he'll have. His education may be funded by the monies raised tonight at the historic hotel on the hill that saw so much history unfold. Dreams do come and go, but those that stay become a quest and this is one of them. So, the money raised will be well spent. It might trickle down through the bureaucracy but eventually it will be used to give money to charities for the neediest of children in the name of education. While the patrons dined on New York Strip Steak in their evening gowns and black ties, upcoming boxers from lightweight to welterweight to heavy and even super heavyweight gave the crowd a taste of what a steady, focused vision was all about. Not so far away, a young life has been touched and a dream has started. And it all began with a mission to help.

Chapter 14

Ken Norton is a survivor. A tested survivor. A fighter, single father, survivor of a near-fatal crash, the ex-Marine exemplifies what perseverance and fortitude are. Known as 'The Jaw Breaker,' or 'The Fighting Marine,' by his fans, Ken was most proud of the title, Dad. A person who had been through a most traumatic episode, he never surrendered and allowed the darker demons to take over. His optimism and 'can do' attitude, which he inherited from his parents and doting Aunt Mary, made him a force not only in the ring but in the world that suddenly changed on that night in 1986.

By 2007, Ken Norton was again active in a venue that he enjoyed—acting. Asked to take the role of the grandfather in the 2008 release of "The Man Who Came Back," he was the perfect pick for the role. The movie, based on a violent labor strike in Texas in 1870 is all but forgotten in history. Thanks to the Louisiana-born director, Glen Pitre, the movie leaves the theater-goer with scenes that call to mind what revenge and hate are all about. It recalls an episode replete in American history with the challenges of the working poor laborers seeking to better their lot and help their families. Despite the rigors imposed by the job, they kept their dignity and demanded a fair wage for an honest days' work. What ensued was horrific. Blood spilled, deceit, revenge and a struggle to right a wrong. A conflict, seen on the big screen, educates the American people of the struggles of just trying to get a decent wage for an honest days' work. The conflicts and test that made their struggle something to appreciate.

Terrible conflicts that test man's capacity to seek justice or get revenge are at the heart of the movie. The bloody encounters shown on the screen in one of the most violent labor disputes will at once mesmerize the moviegoer with a tale of not only bloody revenge but also murder and conspiracy. A calming, wiser and older figure is needed to quell the uprising. Pitre knew that in Ken Norton, he had the right person for the role. As the grandfather, Ken Norton brings his versatile talent to the screen and is at once a calming yet sad character. "I was happy to perform the role and enjoyed being active again." he remarked.

Ken Norton is a person who came back—came back from adversity when confronted with conflicts in his life. From his upbringing in Jacksonville to his marine days and finally to his rise as a professional boxer, he was at once an example of what dreams were made of. It's no wonder that, working with a cast on the set of 'The Man Who Came Back,' he had the support and respect of an impressive cast that included: Armand Assante, Eric Braeden, venerable actor George Kennedy, former model turned actress, Carol Alt, James Patrick Stewart, Jennifer O'Dell, Sean Young and Peter Jason. With the likes of these, Norton could hold his own. Here is a person who could perform on the gridiron, on the canvas toe-to-toe with the best boxers in the world, raise a son single-handedly and perform on a Hollywood set. After all, he had acted in over 20 movies and TV specials. Like all his other challenges, he could handle it and get the job done. Fellow actors knew that Norton, ever the professional, would give his role 100%, as he did with everything in his life. Filmed near the Mexican border town of Del Rio, Texas, Director Pitre, aware of the struggles in the American labor movement, gives justice to this little known but significant bloody conflict. Now, with the years behind him, Ken Norton is able to transcend his talent and give a tour-de-force performance in the role of the sage and venerable grandfather.

As he approaches his 65th birthday, the handsome, ex-heavyweight who ended up on the silver screen despite the accident, is still a person who never took himself too seriously and is most accountable and a delight to have around. His fellow boxers, both opponents and others, have a good deal to express when the subject of Ken Norton comes up.

Earnie Shavers, National AAU heavyweight champion in 1969, had a punch described by Larry Holmes, "harder than Tyson's." He defeated Jimmy Young, Joe Bugner and yes, Ken Norton, losing eventually to the Greatest, Muhammad Ali. In a 15 year span, Shavers had an impressive record of 82-14- with one draw. When asked to comment on his former opponent, Shavers remarked: "Ken was a real fighter and a great champion. He had some unbelievable and tremendous fights with Ali and a very close fight with Larry Holmes. But Ken is also a very good friend. He was an asset to the fight game. The last time he fought Ali, I think he won the fight. Ken went a long way, he was a great fighter—one of the best of the 1970's. The 70's—that was the Golden Age of Boxing."

Aaron Pryor, the 1996 inductee into the International Boxing Hall of Fame and 1980-1985 junior welterweight champion said of Norton: "When I think of my friend, Ken Norton, only two words come to mind—living legend. He has the heart of a warrior and has battled the greatest heavyweights in history. Stepping into the ring with the likes of Muhammad Ali, Larry Holmes, Earnie Shavers, Jerry Quarry, Gerry Cooney and George Foreman, Ken Norton became one this country's most beloved sports figures, ever! He consistently delivered the big battles and the big marquee fights and is one of the top heavyweights of all time." Pryor goes on to explain: "I admire Ken most, though, for his victories outside the ring. Kenneth Howard Norton will always stand tall in my book as a marine, a survivor, a father and a legendary championship fighter. He's done it all and sets the standard for the rest of us International Boxing Hall of Fame inductees to follow." Quite an endorsement from a very respectable and hard-hitting fighter!

Alex Ramos, the young Puerto Rican Bronx teenager running the streets the night of the Norton-Ali fight in 1973 and who snuck into the stadium was inspired by Ken Norton. He fondly recalls: "When I was just a kid, I remember I snuck into Yankee Stadium to see Ken Norton fight. Back in the day, there were great fights at Yankee Stadium and we all loved Ken Norton because he was so tough. Ken inspired me and little did I know that one day I would also be in a fight at Yankee Stadium, where I was presented with the Yankee Pinstripes by George Steinbrenner, Rick Cerrone, Bucky Dent and Dave Winfield which I wore throughout my professional career as the 'Bronx Bomber.'" Ramos went on to a distinguished record, fighting Felix Trinidad, Jr. Don King managed him and got him to the pinnacle of his career. Yet, he never forget that hot summer night in the South Bronx as a youngster looking for something to do and found his hero, Ken Norton. People are inspired by the talents of others and for Ramos, that night at the stadium motivated a young, restless kid into a lucrative and exciting career, thanks to Ken Norton.

Wayne McCullough, a featherweight from Ireland, known as the "Pocket Rocket," had an impressive boxing record of 33 wins and 6 loses. He was the WBC champion when in October, 2000, his boxing career was cut short when a cyst was discovered between his brain and skull. Doctors at UCLA Medical Center determined that the cyst was benign and the dogged, relentless fighter was given the ok to resume his career. Unlike Ken Norton, whose accident occurred after his retirement, McCullough was at the height of his boxing career when the medical scare occurred. He wrote about it in his biography, *Pocket Rocket, Don't Quit*. He fondly recalls meeting Ken Norton in Las Vegas and said: "I met Ken a few years ago at a golf tournament. He struck me as a very intelligent person with a smart sense of humor. He joked with me all day that he couldn't understand what I was saying because of my Irish accent. I told him it wasn't my accent but that I was a leprechaun in disguise!" McCullough was able to maintain his sense of humor and he and Norton were at the Vegas green to lend their voice and support for a fundraising event.

Perhaps the most famous trainer in recent boxing history is Angelo Dundee. Born in Philadelphia as Angelo Mirena to Italian immigrant parents, Dundee worked with some of the best fighters of the late 20th century: Ali, Sugar Ray Leonard, Jose Napoles, George Foreman, Jimmy Ellis, Carmen Basilio and Luis Rodriguez. With his wife Chris, he went to Miami to open the famous 5th Street Gym and launch his long and lustrous career molding some of the best boxers in the business. Ken Norton never trained with Dundee, but they shared a mutual respect from their opposite corners. Said Dundee of Norton: "Ken was top gun. Anything I can do for Kenny, I will. Kenny is a very good guy." Dundee knows boxing and knows what a good fighter has to have both internally and externally. His respect for Norton is shared with many of the greats of the sport, both past and present. Because of Dundee's expertise in the ring, he was asked to consult and train actor Russell Crowe in his role of Jimmy Braddock in the mega hit movie: 'Cinderella Man'.

Jose Sulaiman, Chairman and President of the WBC and inductee into the International Boxing Hall of Fame, has been an accountable and efficient administrator for more than three decades. Sulaiman reduced the rounds from 15 to 12 in championship bouts and expanded the weight divisions. He was most instrumental in the creation of the World Medical Congress with funding from UCLA Medical Center for the study of brain injury. A friend of promoter Don King, Sulaiman, with the changes in the WBC, has made the sport more accountable for the safety of the fighters. He has known many fighters and when asked to appraise Ken Norton was very pleased to report: "Ken Norton was a thrilling and courageous fighter. Also, a pride of boxing and a good friend. May God bless him always, as the WBC will remember him both as a gentleman and an example for youth both in the ring and his private life." Sulaiman, aware of the public's appetite for gossip, finds in Ken a good role model and a decent guy.

Also, Carol Connors, the two time Oscar nominated song writer, is a big fan of Ken Norton. Who can ever forget the soaring, pulsating song she wrote for 'Rocky I', "Gonna Fly Now." As Rocky Balboa, the loved underdog was slowly gaining confidence and strength, the Connors creation made the movie soar, giving Stallone the coveted Oscar for his tour-de-force role. Connors knows Ken Norton as the real deal and remarked: "In the ring, Ken Norton was a champ. In real life, after all he's been through, you have proven yourself to be an even bigger champ." Connors, like all of Norton's family and friends, knows the sacrifices and dedication that led him to where he is today following the devastating crash. A great professional songwriter and friend, her evaluation of Ken Norton, is right on target. Others have said it well, too.

Jill Diamond, the NABF Women's Division Chairperson and WBC Championship Committee and Chair of World Boxing Cares, is a person who knows how little monetary consideration is given to female boxers. Her distinguished resume includes work in music composition and music director for TV. But personal tragedy gave her a different avenue to escape. Her husband died after a protracted battle with colon cancer in 2002. She looked for an escape. She found it in boxing. An article by Robert Mladinich in *The Sweet Sciences* dated September 24, 2006, states: "the commitment of most women boxers is astounding, especially when you consider how little money they make. For many of them, boxing represents something so much more than a vocation. Their devotion to the game is very inspiring to me." Diamond, an Emmy award winner for her work in music direction and composition, immersed herself in boxing after her actor husband, Don Chastain, died. Once she began training at Michale Olajide Sr's International Gym in Manhattan, she felt right at home. Traveling to Los Angeles, she put together a goodwill mission. The Mladinich article goes on to explain: 'She escorted championship fighters, such as Erik 'The Terrible' Morales and Genaro Hernandez to the Children's Hospital of the City of Angels. They brought a message of hope and support from Jose Sulamain as well as gift bags donated by Alberto Reyes and a WBC lifetime membership for the children. Diamond adds: "The support that I received for this project blew me away. The sanctioning bodies are so often maligned, so it's unfortunate that the general public doesn't get to see things like this." Indeed, the program is now considered in over 163 affiliated countries. Such is the work that a host of boxers have signed on: Bernard Hopkins, Wayne McCullough, Laila Ali,

DeMarcus Corley, Alex Ramos, Gerry Cooney, Vtali Klitschko, Lennox Lewis, Floyd Mayweather Jr., Brian Adams, Derric Rossy, Thulane Malinga, Jeff French, John Stracey, Luisito Espinosa and Kostya Tszyu.

After a visit to the hospital, the article sums up the boxers overall assessment. Morales and Hernandez, accompanying Diamond said it best: "It is sad, but at the same time of great importance to come see these children that are struggling with their lives. In all truth, everything I saw touched me profoundly. I'm grateful to have been invited. Battles in the ring don't compare to the situation of these sick children and premature newborns. Nobody knows if they'll make it. The illnesses suffered by these children really scare you and make you truly concerned about what can happen to people at an early age." Diamond recalls that the sick children were overjoyed at the attention and when they posed with the fighters, "the staff was knocked out by how much fun everyone had." It was a bittersweet journey for Diamond. When asked how she felt about boxers who had sustained injuries, she mentioned Ken Norton and remarked: "Ken Norton is the full package—smart, funny, powerful and bigger than life. He's a star in a dark sky; a guiding light for all to follow." Quite an endorsement from a woman who has had her share of life's ups and downs and, like Norton, refused to surrender and has gotten on with her life.

Ken Norton is indeed a tested survivor. Jill Diamond, the young widow needing to make a major adjustment to life's challenges, looked to Ken Norton as a person who has been through a crisis and still came out on top. His struggles to regain his life after his accident and his refusal to give up, gave Diamond and others the incentive to move on. Using their talents, people such as Diamond and Norton now have lent their names and presence to a host of venues for the less fortunate. It takes a special person to show up at a hospice to see a dying friend, to take part in the Macy's Parade for a charitable organization, to participate in Fight Night for children in need and to take a proactive stance in the cause of others. These are what made Ken Norton from the start, the 'guiding light to follow,' as Jill Diamond aptly expressed. Whether it was in his hometown or on the national or international stage, Ken Norton was there. Interspersed with many aspects of our lives, we are reminded how vulnerable and unpredictable life itself can be. In a split second on that California freeway, life, as he knew it, changed forever. Without knowing it or questioning why, he faced the grim realities of life and dealt with it, crisis after crisis. For Ken Norton, his survival instinct took over. He wouldn't let the dark side of life take hold and refused to quit. He was no quitter. His story enriches our lives and makes us stronger in temperament and spirit. A story of survival, hope and vision, it resonates with us and gives us the strength to move on.

About the Authors

Born in Wood River, Illinois, Donald Hennessey Jr. now resides in Jacksonville Illinois. Home of the Internationally Known Boxer Ken Norton. For more than 2 decades Hennessey has worked in business management in one form or another. Hennessey received his doctorate in 2004. Hennessey first met Mr. Norton when he was 11 years old and started working with him about 8 years ago. First as his Midwest liaison, and now as his manager. Most important is the friendship Hennessey and Norton share, Hennessey claims Norton as his second dad. He is currently working on authoring his Autobiography, tentatively title *"To Hell and Back"*

Born in Troy, New York, John V. Amodeo now lives in the Hell's Kitchen area of Manhattan. For three decades Amodeo worked for the NYC public school system as assistant principal; now retired from that post, he is an adjunct professor of political science and US history at Mercy College. Amodeo exercises his love for NY as a part time tour guide. His first book, *'Voices of Hell's Kitchen,'* was a fictional account of the myriad personalities of his neighborhood. He is currently co-authoring a biography of Pittsburgh boxer, Rayco Saunders in forthcoming, *'Blessed or Cursed.'*

See 1stWorld Books at:

www.1stWorldPublishing.com

See our classic collection at:

www.1stWorldLibrary.com

CPSIA information can be obtained
at www.ICGtesting.com
Printed in the USA
BVHW08075730072I
612896BV00008B/962

9 781421 891200